1808

THE HEART OF
HENRI NOUWEN

Also by Henri Nouwen

*Books noted are available from The Crossroad Publishing Company.

THE HEART OF HENRI NOUWEN

HIS WORDS OF BLESSING

EDITED BY

Rebecca Laird &
Michael J. Christensen

A Crossroad Book
The Crossroad Publishing Company
New York

The editors thank The Crossroad Publishing Company for permission to reprint selections from the following works: *In the Name of Jesus: Reflections on Christian Leadership* (1989, 2002); *Beyond the Mirror: Reflections on Death and Life* (1990, 2001); *Life of the Beloved: Spiritual Living in a Secular World* (1992, 2002); *Here and Now: Living in the Spirit* (1994); *Sabbatical Journey: The Diary of His Final Year* (1998); *Finding My Way Home: Pathways to Life and the Spirit* (2001).

Special thanks also for the assistance of Sue Mosteller, Literary Executrix, Henri Nouwen Literary Trust; Gabrielle Earnshaw, Archivist, Henri Nouwen Archives, University of Toronto; and Wendy Greer, President, Henri Nouwen Society.

The Crossroad Publishing Company
481 Eighth Avenue, Suite 1550, New York, NY 10001

This book is typeset in ITC Stone Informal. The text is set at 12/16.

Printed in the United States of America

Library of Congress Cataloging-in-Publication Data

Nouwen, Henri J. M.
  [Selections. 2003]
  The heart of Henri Nouwen : his words of blessing / edited by Rebecca
  Laird & Michael J. Christensen
    p. cm.
  ISBN 0-8245-1985-X (alk. paper)
  1. Spiritual life – Catholic Church. I. Laird, Rebecca. II. Christensen,
  Michael J. III. Title.
  BX2350.3.N692 2003
  248.4′82–dc21

                                                        2003005482

1 2 3 4 5 6 7 8 9 10   10 09 08 07 06 05 04 03

Contents

A Matter of the Heart

"Guess who's coming to dinner?" I asked my wife, Rebecca, waving a fax from Henri Nouwen in my hand. In response to my invitation issued in early 1996 to lead a retreat for faculty and students at the university where I teach, he informed me that he was on a writing sabbatical, "not far from you," at the guest house of a friend in New Jersey. No, he wasn't taking any speaking engagements this year, "but I'd love to have dinner with you and Rebecca."

Henri was my teacher at Yale Divinity School from 1979 to 1981. We had kept in touch since then and had compared notes along life's way through correspondence and occasional visits. Through Henri (I rarely call him by his last name, as no one who knew him ever did), I was introduced to eucharistic worship and contemplative spirituality. He taught me how to pray with icons by embracing the image and finding the hidden door. Upon my graduation from Yale, he advised me — a Protestant — to check into a Trappist monastery to "let your mind descend into your heart and there stand before God." It was with Henri that I had processed important life decisions. He favored me by coming to preach to my thirty-member house church in San Francisco, donating generously to the inner city work I was doing with the homeless and persons with AIDS in that city. When I married Rebecca Laird, he sent us a Byzantine icon of Jesus. When a study guide needed to be written for his book *Letters to Marc about Jesus,* Rebecca was tapped for the task. When each of our daughters was born, he sent a guardian angel to hang on the Christmas tree. There is no person in the world who has had more influence on my adult spirituality than Henri Nouwen as a teacher, writer, and spiritual mentor. And I count it a privilege to be numbered among his fifteen hundred closest friends.[1]

Henri arrived for dinner on a rainy July 19, characteristically with flowers in hand. We greeted him at the door and invited him in for an evening of hospitality in Madison, New Jersey. Our three-and-a-half-year-old daughter, Megan, was especially warm and responsive toward Henri and soon was in his lap. Six-year-old Rachel told him that she had seen his picture in the book lying on the coffee table. We reviewed the last decade and a half of life and ministry over fresh salmon and salad, good wine and Starbucks coffee. Henri shared why he now was able to turn down invitations to the White House and various denominational and professional groups. Soon to turn sixty-five, he said he no longer wanted to fly here and there to meet important people, but to spend time with close friends and devote himself to an even more intentional life of prayer, community, ministry, and writing. There was time over dinner to discuss our mutual concerns and areas of interest, including academia, the church in Latin America, AIDS, Russia, Chernobyl, and, of course, the spiritual life.[2]

After dessert, we retired to the basement for lighter conversation and to watch the first half of the opening ceremony of the 1996 Olympic Games. Content to spend the evening with our family, Henri huddled around a tiny television screen with Megan on his lap. During a commercial break, Megan asked a question she'd been asking lately after seeing the "big" buildings of New York City and hearing that God, too, was mysteriously both "big and small." She turned to Henri and asked, "How big is God?" Henri replied, "God is as big as your heart." She continued to probe: "And how big is that?" Henri smiled and gestured with his large hands, "Your heart is big enough to contain the whole world." A good answer, repeated often in our household, especially since Henri's death. Henri could employ imaginative metaphors and hyperbole in a way that engaged three-and-a-half-year-olds (and the spiritually curious) but often baffled Henri's academic peers unused to such emotional, figurative phrases.

But what exactly did he mean by the answer: "God is as big as your heart"? Henri was a practical mystic with prophetic vision who suffered deeply, examined his own heart, and penetrated the sacred heart of God in prayer. His spiritual practice was to bring into his heart the hearts of all people, even his perceived enemies, so that his heart was ever-widening in compassion and increasingly inclusive. Through his life and writings, he continues to ask the cardinal question—how big is your heart?—and to show us how to enlarge its chambers.

Imagine Henri in his white monastic alb, gesturing with his expressive hands, looking you straight in the eyes, and saying Mass from memory yet with fresh passion and depth of feeling: "He took the cup, looked up into heaven and gave You thanks and praise; gave the cup to his disciples and said, take this all of you and drink it. This is the cup of my blood, the blood of the new and everlasting covenant. It is shed for you, and for all people, so that sins will be forgiven. Do this in remembrance of me."

To watch him perform as a priest and caregiver, to hear him speak with passion to large or small crowds, or to read his words in silence is to encounter a depth of feeling and power of insight known only in the heart. The compelling charism of Henri Nouwen that inspired several generations of students, readers of spiritual books, the physically and mentally handicapped, and a loyal public from around the world, was the way that he acted, spoke and wrote from the heart.

Henri knew how to engage spiritual affections in the deepest part of a person by addressing the questions of the heart: *What do I fear? What do I love? What gives me joy? What brings me peace?* He knew that the heart's affections were deeper than conscious feelings, have objects and relations that shape beliefs, and dispose us to certain kinds of behavior. Like the human heart muscle that pumps blood to enliven the limbs and organs, the spiritual heart nourishes beliefs and behavior. Prior to cognitive beliefs and practices, the heart knows, trusts, values, and seeks truth. The Latin word *credo,* which we translate today as "I believe" originally meant, "I give my heart to." What you give your heart to reveals more of who you are than what you profess to believe and practice.

The word "heart" itself appears constantly in his published works.[3] Since his death in 1996, a video production titled *Straight to the Heart: The Life of Henri Nouwen* has been released. Two academic courses listed as "A Theology of Heart" at St. Francis Xavier University in Canada and "A Matter of the Heart: The Spirituality of Henri Nouwen" at Drew University in the United States have been taught. Aptly, this selection of Henri's finest writing is entitled *The Heart of Henri Nouwen*. Every summary or anthology of Henri's work, it seems, evokes his eucharistic heart of communion and blessing.

—M.J.C.

The Eucharistic
Movement of Heart

The physical heart in the human body is a central muscle with four chambers that receive and transport oxygen-rich blood to the rest of the body. This amazing fist-sized organ recycles about two thousand gallons of lifeblood in a fourfold rhythm—beat, pump, receive, send—at least a hundred thousand times a day. It helps to envision Henri's heart as a four-chambered spiritual muscle constantly beating to the rhythm of life, pumping life-giving blood into the chamber of God's presence, receiving the sufferings of the world into the "oxygen-rich" presence of God in prayer, and sending blood back out to enliven and renew the rest of the spiritual body of Christ in an ongoing cycle: beat, pump, receive, send.

Henri's human heart served him well until an unexpected massive heart attack took his life on September 21, 1996. In God's gracious timing, this wandering prophet and priest died in his homeland of The Netherlands while his family was nearby. Yet it is Henri's spiritual heart that this book celebrates. Since it was Henri's practice for almost forty years to celebrate Communion daily, whether alone or with others, his spiritual heart was essentially a eucharistic heart. (Remember, the word "Eucharist" means "thanksgiving.")

Henri's spiritual heart chambers correspond to the fourfold eucharistic formula in classic Christianity— took, blessed, broke, and gave. In the eucharistic prayer during Mass, the bread is taken or chosen, held up and blessed, broken, and given to feed the faithful. As Henri embodied these eucharistic movements of the heart, his life became spiritual bread and wine, body and blood, for others.

The selections chosen for this volume are organized, appropriately, under the active imperatives: *Choose, Bless, Break, Give.* Each section is introduced with a short biographical essay and some suggestions on how best to savor these readings.

GOD LOOKS UPON THE HEART

Before you read the selections, it may help to understand what Henri, who was both priest and scholar, meant biblically, theologically, and spiritually when he used the word "heart" in his writings.

In all faith traditions, true beliefs, right actions, and proper ritual are important and determinant for religious identity and faithfulness. For Henri Nouwen, *spirituality* was more important than any particular religion, and spirituality was a personal matter of the heart. Is your heart open or closed, contrite or stubborn, soft like a pillow or hard like a stone? The sacrifice or offering God desires is an open, clean, broken, and contrite heart (Ps. 51:17).

The prophet Ezekiel spoke of the transformative possibility of turning a "heart of stone into a heart of flesh." The Psalmist cried out: "Create in me a clean heart, O God, and put a new and right spirit within me." Spiritual formation is the spiritual awakening, purification, growth, and development of a divine heart in the body of a human being, lived out in community and service in the world.

In his standard course, "Introduction to the Spiritual Life," Henri devoted a full lecture to what is meant by "heart."

Biblically, the term "heart" rarely refers to the physical organ (perhaps only in 1 Sam. 25:37 and 2 Kings 9:24, when the heart stops beating). Generally, it is meant as a metaphor for the spiritual life. Specifically, in biblical psychology, the heart is the spiritual organ of the core self: the inner spring of personal life and motivation; the deep source of all desires, thoughts, and choices; the center and seat of the emotions, intellect, and will.[4]

Although Henri delineated these three functional aspects in his course, he focused more on the inner "heart" — the core self or human spirit that belongs only to God. What he means by heart is the "center of our being where God comes to dwell with us and bring us the divine gifts of trust, hope and love." The mind tries to understand reasons, grasp problems, distinguish truth from falsehood, and probe the mysteries of life. "The heart allows us to enter into relationships and experience that we are sons and daughters of God."[5] In the hidden place of the heart, known intimately by God, a divine penetration and human response occur. "Our hearts are restless until they find their rest in Thee," says Augustine. "Within the heart," says Henri, "human beings meet God's word" directly and decisively, which results in conversion and transformation.[6]

Both biblically and theologically, then, the heart is the center for feeling, thinking, and deciding. It represents the total human being at the core. This is why the greatest commandment is to love God with all one's heart, soul, mind, and strength (Deut. 6:5 and Luke 10:27) — that is, with one's whole self. When ancient Israel required a king, God's prophet chose and anointed an unlikely shepherd boy, without royal blood or proper appearance, but with a good and right heart. "For humans judge by outward appearance, but the Lord looks upon the heart" (1 Sam. 16:7).[7]

TOUCHED BY ETERNITY

Spiritually or mystically, according to Henri, "our heart—the center of our being—is a part of God."[8] It is that sacred space within us "where God dwells and we are invited to dwell with God."[9] More than the physical organ that points to its spiritual metaphor, the heart is the "central and unifying organ of our personal life."[10] It is that place "where time touches eternity, where earth and heaven meet, where God's Word becomes human flesh."[11] It is the primordial access point to God, "where there are no divisions or distractions and where we are totally one."[12] There, in the place of the heart, infinite divinity and finite humanity are spiritually united.

In his article "The Trusting Heart and the Primacy of the Mystical Life," Henri records what he learned from Père Thomas of the L'Arche Community in France about the heart: "It is the place of trust, a trust that can be called faith, hope, or love—depending on how it is being manifested.... It is not so much the ability to think, to reflect, to plan, or to produce that makes us different from the rest of creation, but the ability to trust." He goes on to explain that physically and psychologically our hearts respond to and relate to objects in our environment long before our cognitive thinking and conscious moral choices develop. The human infant, for example, responds to a mother's milk and food with complete trust. "It is the [trusting] heart that makes us truly human."[13]

But how does the primacy of the heart relate to cognitive beliefs, religious feelings, and moral choices? Are not right beliefs/worship (*orthodoxy*), right affections (*orthopathos*), and right actions (*orthopraxis*) just as important as a right heart (*orthocardia*)? It was Henri's deep conviction that every human being is "born in intimate communion with the God who created us in love. We belong to God from the moment of our conception. Our heart is that divine gift

18

which allows us to trust not just God but also our parents, our family, ourselves, and our world." Before there is *original sin* there is *original blessing* — our natural and primordial communion with God. Thus, "very small children have a deep, intuitive knowledge of God, a knowledge of the heart, that sadly is often obscured and even suffocated by the many [intellectual] systems of thought we gradually acquire. Handicapped people, who have such a limited ability to learn, can let their heart speak easily and thus reveal a mystical life that for many intelligent people seems unreachable."[14]

The primacy of the heart over intellectual needs for systems and methods also applies to the spectrum of human affections, according to Henri: "The heart is much wider and deeper than our affections. It is before and beyond the distinctions between sorrow and joy, anger and lust, fear and love. It is the place where all is one in God, the place where we truly belong, the place from which we come and to which we always yearn to return."[15]

Does the spirituality of the heart also transcend moral distinctions between right and wrong? "Much church discussion today focuses on morality: premarital sex, divorce, homosexuality, birth control, abortion, etc.," Henri observes. "But when the moral life gets all the attention, we are in danger of forgetting the primacy of the mystical life, which is the life of the heart."[16] Or, as the thirteenth-century Sufi poet Rumi wrote:

> Out beyond ideas of wrong and right,
> there is a field. I'll meet you there.

Henri's life was about meeting God and others in that transcendent "field" of beauty, love, and celebration.

—M.J.C.

The Divine Heart

"I am called," says Henri, "to enter into the sanctuary of my own being where God has chosen to dwell." There, in the cave of the heart, in the presence of God in prayer, "deep speaks to deep" and "heart speaks to heart." In kneeling before God, embracing the divine heart, and listening to the depth of one's own being, one begins to see and hear things from a divine source. Contemplating the intimacy of the embrace between father and son in Rembrandt's painting *The Return of the Prodigal Son,* Henri writes: "I have to kneel before the Father, put my ear against his chest and listen, without interruption, to the heartbeat of God.... Then, and only then, can I say carefully and very gently what I hear." Henri called this vocation, which he best understood in the final few years of his life, the call to "speak from eternity into time,"[17] which is the fruit of prayerfulness more than the result of any particular form of prayer.

In his university courses, Henri often repeated Tolstoy's story of the three isolated monks who managed to pray truly and deeply from the heart without the theological benefit of a proper religious education: "Three Russian monks lived on a faraway island. Nobody ever went there, but one day their bishop decided to make a pastoral visit. When he arrived he discovered that the monks didn't even know the Lord's Prayer. So he spent all his time and energy teaching them the Our Father and then left, satisfied with his pastoral work. But when his ship had left the island and was back in the open sea, he suddenly noticed the three hermits walking on the water — in fact, they were running after the ship! When they reached it they cried, 'Dear Father, we have forgotten the prayer you taught us.' The bishop, overwhelmed by what he was seeing and hearing, said, 'But, dear brothers, how then do you pray?' They answered, 'Well, we just say, "Dear God, there are three of us and there are three of you, have mercy on us!"' The bishop, awestruck by their sanctity and simplicity, said, 'Go back to your island and be at peace.'"[18]

The point of Tolstoy's story, of course, is that the prayerfulness of the heart is deeper and ultimately more important than the particular words that are prayed. An untrained person with a simple and humble heart may pray more effectively from the heart than one who knows how to use the appropriate theological language and proper forms of prayer.

In *Heart Speaks to Heart,* a devotional book about the deep suffering of the human heart, Henri confesses his chronic struggle with shame, depression, unfulfilled needs, and perceived rejection in light of his heart's primordial connection with the wounded heart of God. The book contains three heartfelt prayers offered to the "sacred heart of Jesus," which also suffers. He writes in the Prologue: "The pain of having to leave Daybreak for a time, and not being there during Holy Week and Easter, cut very deep in my heart. At some moments, it seemed hardly tolerable. But as I looked up to Jesus, washing his disciples' feet and sharing with them his body and blood, . . . I began to write to Jesus—from heart to heart."[19]

In the first prayer, he recognizes the all-inclusive heart of Christ that welcomes all persons home: "Your heart does not distinguish between rich and poor, friend and enemy, female and male, slave and free, sinner and saint. Your heart is open to receive anyone with total, unrestricted love."[20]

His second prayer is an identification of his own broken heart with divine woundedness and suffering: "O Jesus, I look into my own heart and at my own hands. There, too, I find blood. My own heart seems like a microcosm of the world of violence and destruction in which I live. . . . I look at your pierced side and see blood flowing from your heart . . . to heal my broken heart and the broken hearts of every man and woman in every time and place."[21]

In his third prayer he recognizes that the wounded heart of God's love is one with his own heart and with the broken heart of the world: "Whenever I touch your broken heart, I touch the hearts of your broken people, and whenever I touch the hearts of our broken people, I touch your heart. Your broken heart and the broken heart of the world are one. . . . Here I am, Lord, take my heart and let it become a heart filled with your love."[22]

Henri's sense of the primacy of the human heart and its mystical identification with the sacred heart of Jesus is not only grounded in Roman Catholic devotion, but is related to the deep understanding of his spiritual teacher, Thomas Merton.

Thomas Merton (1915–68) referred to the human heart, the deepest part of the human person, as *le point vierge* (the virgin point) — "the center of our nothingness where, in apparent despair, one meets God—and is found completely in His mercy."[23]

Le point vierge, the virgin point of the spirit, is said to be an originating still point outside of time and space, which is at one with God and which constitutes our true identity, our true beginning and end. What Merton understood and passed on through his writings to Henri was that God and humanity encounter each other in the human heart, the consciousness of which produces mystical insight into the essential nature of reality. For example, Merton's sudden and overwhelming realization in the shopping district at the corner of Fourth and Walnut in Louisville on March 18, 1958—that he loved all these people "walking around shining like the sun" — could be expressed only by employing the untranslatable term *Le point vierge:* "Then it was as if I suddenly saw the secret beauty of their hearts, the depths of their hearts where neither sin nor desire nor self-knowledge can reach, the core of their reality, the person that each one is in God's eyes.... Again, that expression, *le point vierge* (I cannot translate it) comes in here. At the center of our being is a point of nothingness which is untouched by sin and by illusion, a point of pure truth, a point or spark which belongs entirely to God.... This little point...is the pure glory of God in us....It is like a pure diamond, blazing with the invisible light of heaven. It is in everybody."[24]

Merton understood that our own access to God was connected to the penetrating and penetrable hearts of all God's people. And through Merton, Henri came to experience and understand the importance of the place of the heart in contemplative prayer and the way of the heart as communion with God.

THE WAY OF THE HEART
IN EASTERN CHRISTIANITY

Henri's spiritual use of the word "heart" can be understood in the context of his immersion in Eastern Orthodox theology and the Russian hesychast tradition.[25] He drank deeply from the well of the Desert Fathers and Mothers and learned from the sayings of these monks and hermits of the third and fourth centuries. Their stories, as cited in Henri's *The Way of the Heart* and his *Introduction to Desert Wisdom: Sayings of the Desert Fathers,* illustrate how to pray with simplicity and passion to ignite the spiritual fire within. For example, when Abba Lot went to see Abba Joseph to ask what else he should do besides prayer, fasting, silence, meditation, and keeping his thoughts clean, the old man "stood up and stretched out his hands toward heaven, and his fingers became like ten torches of flame. And he said: If you wish, you can become all flame."[26]

From Macarius of Egypt he learned that the "chief task of the athlete [that is, the monk] is to enter into his heart" and to mine the depths of God: "Within the heart are unfathomable depths. There are reception rooms and bedchambers in it, doors and porches, and many offices and passages....The heart is Christ's palace: there Christ the King comes to take His rest, with the angels and the spirits of the saints, and He dwells there, walking within it and placing His Kingdom there."[27]

From the nineteenth-century Russian mystic Theophan the Recluse Henri learned that to pray is to "descend with the mind into the heart, and there to stand before the face of the Lord, ever-present, all-seeing, within you."[28] This form of mystical prayer transcends the boundaries of consciousness" into mystical meditation, contemplation, and beatific vision. This state of grace, Bishop Kalistos Ware explains, "is a captivity of the mind and of the entire vision by a spiritual object so overpowering that all outward things are forgotten, and wholly absent from the consciousness." The practice of standing before God with mind in heart "may be accompanied by words, or it may be 'soundless': sometimes we speak to God, sometimes we simply remain in his presence, saying nothing, but conscious that He is near us." Whether listening in silence or engaged in quiet conversation, "this notion of being 'with the mind in the heart" constitutes a cardinal principle in the Orthodox doctrine of prayer.[29]

Henri also read the classic Russian tale *The Way of a Pilgrim* and learned from the *staretz* (Russian hermit) that there was a way of "praying without ceasing" (1 Thess. 5:17) and thus to be ever conscious of the spirit of God within. The practice is called the "Prayer of the Heart" or the "Jesus Prayer" and consists of repeating the words "Lord Jesus Christ, have mercy on me" to the rhythm of one's heartbeat.[30]

Henri was challenged by Isaac the Syrian to enter the "treasure chamber" of the heart in order to gain entrance to the kingdom of God within. "The ladder to this Kingdom is hidden in your soul," Isaac wrote. We descend first into the depths of the heart, there find the Spirit of Christ at rest. Then, together with Christ, we ascend the ladder—rung by rung, higher and higher—until we are one with Christ and one with all creation.[31]

In *The Way of the Heart,* Henri articulates the ancient practice of "unceasing prayer," which allows the mind to descend into the heart to find peace and rest in God. He structures his desert reflections around the story of Arsenius, a Roman senator who became a desert monk in the fourth century. "While still living in the palace," Henri quotes his source, "Abba Arsenius prayed to God these words, 'Lord, lead me in the way of salvation.' And a voice came saying to him, 'Arsenius, flee the world...be silent, pray always.'" These three movements of the heart — withdrawal to solitude, contemplative silence, and unceasing prayer — characterize the spirituality of the desert, which is the wisdom source and tradition that formed the heart of Henri Nouwen.

In his own spiritual practice of these disciplines, Henri came to know himself as "God's beloved."[32] Following the classical stages of spiritual development—conversion, illumination, purgation, and unification — and with the guidance of spiritual directors, he was drawn from enlightenment to embodiment in conformity to the divine image within. Increasingly, he was able to enter into the heart of God and mind of Christ and to see things spiritually from a divine perspective. The one who prays to God from the heart, in silence, Henri says, crediting his mentor, Thomas Merton, "will come to recognize the presence of God in the many ideas, meetings, books, people, and events along the way."[33]

It is our hope that you will recognize the presence of God in these pages. Henri's spiritual heart is still pumping life through his writings into those who will allow their own soft and broken hearts to be turned toward the source of love.

—M.J.C.

THE HEART OF
HENRI NOUWEN

Choose

How do we get in touch with our chosenness when we are surrounded by rejections? I have already said that this involves a real spiritual struggle. Are there any guidelines in this struggle? Let me try to formulate a few.
                                                    —*Life of the Beloved*, 48

It was Henri's deepest conviction that he (and every person) was chosen *by God before the foundations of the earth to be a child of God and called "my beloved in whom I am well pleased" (Luke 3:22). His most joyful task and greatest gift was to remind himself and others of their true identify and purpose. "My friends," he would often say, "I tell you that we are loved with a 'first love' even before we are born."*[34]

Henri also believed that the spiritual life is not a given but a gift that we must choose to accept and live in the guiding light of God's love. We have the freedom to choose and the power to change our perspectives. We can choose to pray daily, serve freely, and join others in spiritual community.

When Henri says, "dare to believe that you are beloved before you were born," he speaks words born not of enthusiasm but of experience.

Henri Josef Machiel Nouwen was born on January 23, 1932, in Nijkerk, The Netherlands, after three days and nights of hard labor. Many prayed during the long wait and feared for the lives of both the mother and her first-born. Both survived, and they drew close from a shared depth of religious devotion and aesthetic sensibility. Maria Nouwen-Ramselaar was a great reader with interests in literature, languages, and mysticism. After she died of cancer in 1978, Henri wrote In Memoriam about her life and death. He recalled, "I see her waving from the platform as the train rolled away from the station, making her figure smaller and smaller. Always there was a smile and a tear, joy and sadness. From the moment of my birth when her tears merged with smiles, it has always been that way."

After her death, Henri sent the manuscript of In Memoriam to his father but received no response, no thanks, no *acknowledgment. This pained him greatly. Henri's father, Laurent, was an ambitious and accomplished professor of tax law at the University of Nijmegen, but not one to lavish praise or affirmation. The lack of response to Henri's book was the kind of action easily brushed off by some, but for someone with Henri's exquisite sensitivities and need for affirmation, it dealt a body blow.*

From earliest childhood, Henri asked his parents, "Do you really love me?" He craved reassurance that he was loved by family and friends, and ultimately by God.[35] *His mother loved him deeply and he knew it, yet later in life she apologized to Henri for strictly following the advice of a child-rearing philosophy that children's strong wills should be broken by restricting food and physical touch. Henri remembered always being hungry and asking for affirmation as a child. His father, a good Dutch father with high standards by all accounts, expected his son to achieve and lead, and Henri did. He became a tenured professor at Yale and then Professor of Divinity at Harvard University. He wrote more than forty books on the spiritual life that continue to be bestsellers, and he achieved these successes in English, his second language.*

Only late in both of their lives did Henri and his father begin to understand each other as driven men striving for thing things that would not ultimately satisfy. After

Henri's own death at the age of sixty-four, his ninety-four-year-old father wrote, "I was proud of [Henri's] success. When he left Holland to go to the States he had nothing— no money, no relations, nothing. When he had money, he gave it away. He was a very devoted son but also very human. I miss him a lot. He was always writing and visiting. He had much of his mother in him, eager, always working."

Henri's professional successes failed in creating a sense of belonging. He moved from school to school, staying ten years at Yale, departing for South America, and returning to Harvard for three years before leaving academics for Daybreak, a community that offers a home for people with mental disabilities in Richmond Hill, Ontario. Daybreak become his heart's home—even though he traveled constantly—for the remaining years of his life. At Daybreak, Henri matured from a Dutch Catholic priest devoted to Jesus and activist academic into the pastor of an ecumenical, interfaith community who found God was most available in the weak and mystery-shrouded parts of his life.

For this restless man of great depth and vulnerability, his life was a parable of coming home to his core identity. He needed to do what he had encouraged others to do: "Claim the love of God, the love that transcends all judgments." Henri wrote about his own spiritual home-coming in The Return of the Prodigal Son. Inspired by Rembrandt's painting of the prodigal son, Henri traveled to the Hermitage in St. Petersburg (Leningrad) to see the original. For several days he sat before the massive painting and reflected upon it. As he viewed the painting, Henri sensed an invitation to join in the drama in a spiritual way. He saw the compassionate father holding the wandering son close to his heart and knew that the truest home is found in that divine embrace. There a wandering soul can hear the guiding heartbeat born of eternal love.

Henri wrote, "The spiritual life is one of the constant choice. One of the more important choices is the choice of the people with whom we develop close intimate relationships." He found that he could best choose, dare, and claim his belovedness within the boundaries of intentional community. His final years spent in Daybreak were hard and healing ones. There he discovered that it was time for him to change his self-understanding. He was no longer the wandering prodigal or the resentful older brother. Instead, his final calling was to become like the welcoming Father: one who would offer a hospitable heart and open embrace to others who had wandered long and far in search of a place to call home.

The following selections from Henri's books emphasize our ability to choose how we will view ourselves and others.

This first section is subdivided into three smaller group-ings. The initial grouping, "Affirm the Truth," echoes the truth that you are chosen by God, loved, and able to reflect that love through your own life. The second grouping, "Seek Community," deals with the realities of friendship, fam-ily, and intentional communities that teach us how much we need each other. The third grouping, "Give Thanks," emphasizes the choices we all regularly make between gratitude and indifference, joy and sorrow.

These selections are meant to be read slowly. It will be best if you sample a few and save time to reflect upon them before reading on. If your situation allows, try reading the shorter pieces aloud. Let the words resonate deeply.

—R.L.

AFFIRM THE TRUTH

First of all, you have to keep unmasking the world about you for what it is: manipulative, controlling, power-hungry, and, in the long run, destructive. The world tells you many lies about who you are, and you simply have to be realistic enough to remind your-self of this. Every time you feel hurt, offended, or rejected, you have to dare to say to yourself: "These feelings, strong as they may be, are not telling me the truth about myself. The truth, even though I cannot feel it right now, is that I am the chosen child of God, precious in God's eyes, called the Beloved from all eternity, and held safe in an everlasting embrace."

—*Life of the Beloved*, 48

You are my beloved

There was that voice, that incredible voice: "You are my beloved son and on you my favor rests." That's the voice at the Jordan River, where Jesus heard and believed that he was the beloved of God on whom God's favor rests. It was as the beloved that Jesus lived his life even in front of the demon. The evil spirit said to him, "Prove that you are the beloved by changing stones into bread and becoming relevant. Prove that you are the beloved by being spectacular and throwing yourself down from the Temple to be saved by God's angels. You'll be in the news and on TV so everyone can see how wonderful you are! Prove that you are the beloved by having power and influence so you can control the situation." But Jesus answered, "I don't have to prove anything. I *am* the beloved because that's the voice I heard in the Jordan River. I know that I am the beloved. I have heard the words, 'You are my beloved. You are my beloved.'" Jesus believed the words and he knew who he was. He lived his whole life as the beloved of God. His spirit was imbued with Love. And Jesus died well because he knew he was going to God and he would soon send his Spirit of Love to his friends. "It is good for you that I leave," he said, "because unless I leave, I cannot send my Spirit, who will lead you to the full communion, to the full truth, to the full betrothal." With that Holy Spirit he knew that his beloved apostles would live better, happier lives.

This vision is not just about Jesus. It is also about you and me. Jesus came to share his identity with you and to tell you that you are the beloved sons and daughters of God. Just for a moment try to enter this enormous mystery, that you, like Jesus, are the beloved daughter or the beloved son of God. This is the truth. Furthermore, your belovedness preceded your birth. You were the beloved before your father, mother, brother, sister, or church loved you or hurt you. You are the beloved because you belong to God from all eternity.

God loved you before you were born, and God will love you after you die. In Scripture God says, "I have loved you with an everlasting love." This is a very fundamental truth of your identity. This is who you are whether you feel it or not. You belong to God from eternity to eternity. Life is just a little opportunity for you during a few years to say, "I love you, too."   —*Finding My Way Home*, 130–32

Your life is very special

If you dare to believe that you are beloved before you are born, you may suddenly realize that your life is very, very special. You become conscious that you were sent here just for a short time, for twenty, forty, or eighty years, to discover and believe that you are a beloved child of God. The length of time doesn't matter. You are sent into this world to believe in yourself as God's chosen one and then to help your brothers and sisters know that they also are beloved sons and daughters of God who belong together. You're sent into this world to be a people of reconciliation. You are sent to heal, to break down the walls between you and your neighbors, locally, nationally, and globally. Before all the distinctions, the separations, and the walls built on foundations of fear, there was unity in the mind and heart of God. Out of that unity, you are sent into this world for a little while to claim that you and every other human

41

being belongs to that same God of Love who lives from eternity to eternity.   —*Finding My Way Home,* 132

You belong to me

A few years ago I was hit by a car and ended up in the hospital. I was feeling very uncomfortable lying on the gurney, but I didn't have any external injuries to speak of so I thought I would be released to return home. When the doctor finally examined me, he was kind but clear, saying, "You might not live long. There is serious internal bleeding. We will try to operate but we may not succeed."

Suddenly everything changed. Death was right there in the room with me. I realized that this might be the moment of my death. I felt shocked, and there were many thoughts going through my mind until I had a further experience. I had never felt anything like it before because in the midst of my confusion and shock I became very calm, very "at rest," and there was a sort of "embrace of God" that reassured me and gently told me, "Don't be afraid. You are safe. I am going to bring you home. You belong to me, and I belong to you."

I was so amazingly at peace that later that night after the surgery when I woke up in the intensive care unit, I felt extremely disappointed. I asked myself, "What am I doing here and why am I still alive?" I kept wondering what had happened to me. Gradually I realized that perhaps for the first time in my life I had contemplated my death not through the eyes of fear but through the eyes of love. Somehow, if only for a moment, I had known God, felt unconditionally loved, and I had experienced being a lover.

—*Finding My Way Home*, 123–25

The chosenness of others

In this world when you are chosen, you know that somebody else is not chosen. When you are the best, you know that somebody is not the best. When you win and receive a prize, you know there is somebody who lost. But this is not so in the heart of God. If you are chosen in the heart of God, you have eyes to see the chosenness of others. If the Love of God blesses you, you have eyes to see the blessedness of others. The mystery of God's wonderful love is that you come with it into the world and it blesses you whether you know it or not. Your life is in God's universal embrace of the whole human family. So if you look with eyes of faith you discover that you belong to a sacred family. You are son or daughter. You are brother or sister.

You are father or mother in the most deeply spiritual way. This little life brings it all together.

—*Finding My Way Home,* 134

Choose joy

Joy is essential to spiritual life. Whatever we may think or say about God, when we are not joyful, our thoughts and words cannot bear fruit. Jesus reveals to us God's love so that his joy may become ours and that our joy may become complete. Joy is the experience of knowing that you are unconditionally loved and that nothing — sickness, failure, emotional distress, oppression, war, or even death — can take that love away.

Joy is not the same as happiness. We can be unhappy about many things, but joy can still be there because it comes from the knowledge of God's love for us. We are inclined to think that when we are sad we cannot be glad, but in the life of a God-centered person, sorrow and joy can exist together. That isn't easy to understand, but when we think about some of our deepest life experiences, such as being present at the birth of a child or the death of a friend, great sorrow and great joy are often seen to be parts of the same experience. Often we discover the joy in the midst of the sorrow. I remember the most painful times of my life as times in which I became aware of a spiritual reality much larger than myself, a reality that allowed me to live the pain with hope. I dare even to say: "My grief was the place where I found my joy." Still, nothing happens automatically in the spiritual life. Joy does not simply happen to us. We have to choose joy and keep choosing it every day. It is a choice based on the knowledge that we belong to God and have found in God our refuge and our safety and that nothing, not even death, can take God away from us.   —*Here and Now*, 26–27

Pay attention to signs of love

There is an intimate relationship between joy and hope. While optimism makes us live as if someday soon things will go better for us, hope frees us from the need to predict the future and allows us to live in the present, with the deep trust that God will never leave us alone but will fulfill the deepest desires of our heart.

Joy in this perspective is the fruit of hope. When I trust deeply that today God is truly with me and holds me safe in a divine embrace, guiding every one of my steps, I can let go of my anxious need to know how tomorrow will look, or what will happen next month or next year. I can be fully where I am and pay attention to the many signs of God's love within and around me....

I remember once walking along the beach with a friend. We spoke intensely about our relationship, trying hard to explain ourselves to each other and to understand each other's feelings. We were so preoccupied with our mutual struggle that we didn't notice the magnificent sunset spreading a rich spectrum of color over the foam-capped waves breaking on the wide, silent beach.

Suddenly my friend exclaimed: "Look...look at the sun...look." He put his arm around my shoulder, and together we gazed at the shimmering ball of fire vanishing gradually below the horizon of the wide ocean.

At that moment, we both knew about hope and joy.

—*Here and Now,* 33–34

Claim God's love

Can we free ourselves from the need to judge others? Yes...by claiming for ourselves the truth that we are the beloved daughters and sons of God. As long as we continue to live as if we are what we do, what

46

we have, and what other people think about us, we will remain filled with judgments, opinions, evaluations, and condemnations. We will remain addicted to the need to put people and things in their "right" place. To the degree that we embrace the truth that our identity is not rooted in our success, power, or popularity, but in God's infinite love, to that degree can we let go of our need to judge.

"Do not judge, and you will not be judged; because the judgments you give are the judgments you will get" (Matt. 7:1). From this and all the other texts of the Gospel, it becomes clear that God's judgment is not the result of some divine calculation of which we have no part, but the direct reflection of our lack of trust in God's love. If we think of ourselves as the sum total of our successes, popularity, and power we become dependent on the ways we judge and are being judged and end up as victims manipulated by the world. And so we bring judgment on ourselves. Our death will mean not only the end of the exchange of judgments but also the end of ourselves, since we become nothing but the result of what we thought of others and what others thought of us.

Only when we claim the love of God, the love that transcends all judgments, can we overcome all fear of judgment. When we have become completely free from the need to judge others, we will also become completely free from the fear of being judged.

The experience of not having to judge cannot co-exist with the fear of being judged, and the experience of God's non-judgmental love cannot coexist with a need to judge others. That's what Jesus means when he says: "Do not judge, and you will not be judged." The connection between the two sides of this sentence is the same connection that exists between the love of God and the love of neighbor. They cannot be separated. This connection, however, is not simply a logical connection that can be thought through. It is first and foremost a connection of the heart that is made in prayer.   —*Here and Now,* 61–63

Do you love me?

The simple statement "God is love" has far-reaching implications the minute we begin living our lives based on that statement. When God, who has created me, is love and only love, I am loved before any human being loved me.

When I was a small child I kept asking my father and mother: "Do you love me?" I asked that question so often and so persistently that it became a source of irritation to my parents. Even though they assured me hundreds of times that they loved me, I never seemed fully satisfied with their answers and kept on asking the same question. Now, many years later, I realize that I wanted a response they couldn't give. I wanted them to love me with an everlasting love. I know that this was the case because my question, "Do you love me?" was always accompanied by the question, "Do I have to die?" Somehow, I must have known that if my parents would love me with a total, unlimited, unconditional love, I would never die. And so I kept pestering my parents with the strange hope that I would be an exception to the general rule that all people are going to die one day.

Much of our energy goes into the question: "Do you love me?" As we grow older, we develop many more subtle and sophisticated ways of asking that question. We say: "Do you trust me, do you care for me, do you appreciate me, are you faithful to me, will you support me, will you speak well of me, and so on and on." Much of our pain comes from our experience of not having been loved well.

The great spiritual challenge is to discover, over time, that the limited, conditional, and temporal love we receive from parents, husbands, wives, children, teachers, colleagues, and friends is a reflection of the unlimited, unconditional, and everlasting love of God. Whenever we can make that huge leap of faith we will know that death is no longer the end but the gateway to the fullness of the Divine Love.

—*Here and Now*, 77–78

From fatalism to faith

We are always tempted with fatalism. When we say, "Well I have always been impatient; I guess I have to live with it," we are being fatalistic. When we say, "That man never had a loving father or mother; you shouldn't be surprised that he ended up in prison," we speak as fatalists. When we say, "She was terribly abused as a child; how do you expect her to ever have a healthy relationship with a man," we allow fatalism to overshadow us. When we say, "The wars between nations, the starvation of millions of people, the AIDS epidemic, and the economic depression all over the world all prove that there is little reason for hope," we have become victims of fatalism.

Fatalism is the attitude that makes us live as passive victims of exterior circumstances beyond our control.

The opposite of fatalism is faith. Faith is the deep trust that God's love is stronger than all the anonymous powers of the world and can transform us from victims of darkness into servants of light.

After Jesus drove out the demon from a lunatic boy, his disciples asked him: "Why were we unable to cast it out?" Jesus answered: "Because you have little faith. I tell you solemnly, if your faith were the size of a mustard seed, you could say to this mountain, move from here to there and it would move; nothing would be impossible for you" (Matt. 17:19–20).

It is important to identify the many ways in which we think, speak, or act with fatalism and, step by step, to convert them into moments of faith. This movement from fatalism to faith is the movement that will remove the cold darkness from our hearts and transform us into people whose trust in the power of love can, indeed, make mountains move.

—Here and Now, 79–80

Reveal God's faithfulness

To be truthful all human relationships must find their source in God and witness to God's love. One of the most important qualities of God's love is faithfulness. God is a faithful God, a God who fulfills the divine promise and will never let us down. God shows this faithfulness to Abraham and Sarah, Isaac and Rebecca, Jacob and Rachel. God shows this faithfulness to Moses and Aaron and to the people as they move from Egypt to the promised land. But God's faithfulness goes beyond that. God wants not only to be a God *for* us, but also a God *with* us. That happens in Jesus, the Emmanuel who walks with us, talks with us, and dies with us. In sending Jesus to us, God wants to convince us of the unshakeable fidelity of the divine love. Still there is more. When Jesus leaves he says to us, "I will not leave you alone, but will send you the Holy Spirit." The Spirit of Jesus is God *within* us. Here the fullness of God's faithfulness is revealed. Through Jesus, God gives us the divine Spirit so that we can live a God-like life. The Spirit is the breath of God. It is the intimacy between Jesus and his Father. It is the divine communion. It is God's love active within us.

This divine faithfulness is the core of our witness. By our words, but most of all by our lives, we are to reveal God's faithfulness to the world. The world is not interested in faithfulness, because faithfulness does not help in the acquisition of success, popularity, and power. But when Jesus calls us to love one another as he has loved us, he calls us to faithful relationships, not based on the pragmatic concerns of the world, but on the knowledge of God's everlasting love.

Faithfulness, obviously, does not mean sticking it out together to the bitter end. That is no reflection of God's love. Faithfulness means that every decision we make in our lives together is guided by the deep awareness that we are called to be living signs of God's faithful presence among us. And this requires an attentiveness to one another that goes far beyond any formal obligation. —*Here and Now*, 128–29

Claim your belovedness

The spiritual life requires a constant claiming of our true identity. Our true identity is that we are God's children, the beloved sons and daughters of our heavenly Father. Jesus' life reveals to us this mysterious truth. After Jesus was baptized in the Jordan by John, as he was coming up out of the water, he saw the heavens torn apart and the Spirit, like a dove, descending on him. And a voice came from heaven: "You are my Son, the Beloved; my favor rests on you" (Mark 1:10–11). This is the decisive moment of Jesus' life. His true identity is declared to him. He is the Beloved of God. As "the Beloved" he is being sent into the world so that through him all people will discover and claim their own belovedness.

But the same Spirit who descended on Jesus and affirmed his identity as the Beloved Son of God also drove him into the desert to be tested by Satan. Satan asked him to prove his belovedness by changing stones to bread, by throwing himself from the temple tower to be carried by angels, and by accepting the kingdoms of the world. But Jesus resisted these temptations of success, popularity, and power by claiming strongly for himself his true identity. Jesus didn't have to prove to the world that he was worthy of love. He already was the "Beloved," and this Belovedness allowed him to live free from the manipulative games of the world, always faithful to the voice that had spoken to him at the Jordan. Jesus' whole life was a life of obedience, of attentive listening to the One who called him the Beloved. Everything that Jesus said or did came forth from that most intimate spiritual communion. Jesus revealed to us that we sinful, broken human beings are invited to that same communion that Jesus lived, that we are the beloved sons and daughters of God just as he is the Beloved Son, that we are sent into the world to proclaim the belovedness of all people as he was and that we will finally escape the destructive powers of death as he did.   —*Here and Now*, 134–35

Accept God's timing

Each time we claim for ourselves the truth of our belovedness, our lives are widened and deepened. As the beloved our lives stretch out far beyond the boundaries of our birth and death. We do not simply become the beloved at our birth and cease being the beloved at our death. Our belovedness is eternal. God says to us: "I love you with an everlasting love." This love was there before our fathers and mothers loved us, and it will be there long after our friends have cared for us. It is a divine love, an everlasting love, an eternal love.

Precisely because our true identity is rooted in this unconditional, unlimited, everlasting love, we can escape being victimized by our "clock-time." Clock-time is the time we have in this world. That time can be measured in seconds, minutes, hours, days, weeks, months, and years. Our clock-time, *chronos* in Greek, can become an obsession, especially when all that we are is connected with the clock that keeps ticking whether we are awake or asleep.

I have always been very conscious of my clock-time. Often I asked myself: "Can I still double my years?" When I was thirty I said: "I can easily live another thirty!" When I was forty, I mused, "Maybe I am only halfway!" Today I can no longer say that, and my question has become: "How am I going to use the few years left to me?" All these concerns about our clock-time come from below. They are based on the presupposition that our chronology is all we have to live. But looked upon from above, from God's perspective, our clock-time is embedded in the timeless embrace of God. Looked upon from above, our years on earth are not simply *chronos* but *kairos* — another Greek word for time — which is the opportunity to claim for ourselves the love that God offers us from eternity to eternity. And so our short lives, instead of being that limited amount of years to which we must anxiously cling, become that saving opportunity to respond with all of our hearts, souls, and minds to God's love and so become true partners in the divine communion.   —*Here and Now,* 137–39

Possibilities for love

A long time of solitude in a Trappist monastery interrupting a busy life of teaching, the sudden death of my mother interrupting my deepest bond with my family, a confrontation with poverty in Latin America interrupting a rather comfortable life in the North, a call to live with mentally handicapped people interrupting an academic career, the breakage of a deep friendship interrupting a growing sense of emotional safety—such events have forced me over and over again to ask myself the question "Where is God and who is God for me?"

All of these interruptions presented themselves as opportunities to go beyond the normal patterns of daily life and find deeper connections than the previous safeguards of my physical, emotional, and spiritual well-being. Each interruption invited me to look in a new way at my identity before God. Each interruption took something away from me; each interruption offered something new. Beyond the success of teaching was the inner peace of solitude and community; beyond the bond with my mother was the maternal presence of God; beyond the comforts of North America were the smiles of the children of God in Bolivia and Peru; beyond the academic career was the vocation to touch God in those whose minds and bodies are broken; beyond a very nurturing friendship was the communion with a God who asked for every part of my heart. In short, beyond the many "social arrangements" that make for a good life are the many possibilities of a relationship with the God of Abraham and Sarah, Isaac and Rebekah, Jacob, Leah and Rachel, the Father of Jesus, whose name is Love.   —*Beyond the Mirror*, 15–17

I am a child of God

I know now that the words spoken to Jesus when he was baptized are words spoken also to me and to all who are brothers and sisters of Jesus. My tendencies toward self-rejection and self-depreciation make it hard to hear these words truly and let them descend into the center of my heart. But once I have received these words fully, I am set free from my compulsion to prove myself to the world and can live in it without belonging to it. Once I have accepted the truth that I am God's beloved child, unconditionally loved, I can be sent into the world to speak and to act as Jesus did.

The great spiritual task facing me is to so fully trust that I belong to God that I can be free in the world — free to speak even when my words are not received; free to act even when my actions are criticized, ridiculed, or considered useless; free also to receive love from people and to be grateful for all the signs of God's presence in the world. I am convinced

that I will truly be able to love the world when I fully
believe that I am loved far beyond its boundaries.

—Beyond the Mirror, 69–70

Only God knows who we truly are

The big event tonight was the soccer match between
Germany and the Czech Republic. My father and I
had an early dinner so we could watch it on TV.

I will always remember the Czech goalkeeper. He
played an astonishingly good game; many times he
prevented the Germans from scoring. His agility,
courage, foresight, and iron nerves made him in
my eyes the great hero. But in overtime, when the
match was 1–1, he couldn't hold on to the ball that
the German player shot into his hands, so he was the
reason why the Germans, not the Czechs, received
the European Cup from Queen Elizabeth. He will
be remembered not as a hero but as the man who
failed to give the Czech Republic its victory. While the
Germans were dancing on the field, embracing one
another, crying with joy, and raising their arms vic-
toriously, this talented goalkeeper sat against one of
the goalposts, his head buried in his knees. Nobody
was there with him. He was the loser.

I feel deeply moved by the image of the defeated goalkeeper. All his great performances will be forgotten, in light of the one mistake that cost the Czechs the greatly desired European Cup. I often wonder about this "final mistake." After a long and fruitful life, one unhappy event, one mistake, one sin, one failure can be enough to create a lasting memory of defeat. For what will we be remembered? For our many acts of kindness, generosity, courage, and love, or for the one mistake we made toward the end? "Yes, he was fabulous, but he failed." "Yes, she was a saintly person, but she sinned." "Yes, they were great, but at the end they disappointed us."

Sometimes I think about dying before the great mistake! What if the "saints" had lived longer and had not been able to keep the ball in their hands at the final moment? Would such a small mistake have brought their saintliness to nothing? It frightens me to think this way. I realize that finally human beings are very fickle in their judgments. God and only God knows us in our essence, loves us well, forgives us fully, and remembers us for who we truly are.

—Sabbatical Journey, 189

SEEK COMMUNITY

Second, you have to keep looking for people and places where your truth is spoken and where you are reminded of your deepest identity as the chosen one.

—*Life of the Beloved*, 49–50

Take the risk of friendship

My need for friendship is great, greater than seems "normal." When I think about the pains and joys of my life, they have little to do with success, money, career, country, or church, but everything to do with friendships. My friendship with Nathan and Sue proves that clearly. The moments of ecstasy and agony connected with both of them mark my nine years at Daybreak.

I have felt rejected as well as supported, abandoned as well as embraced, hated as well as loved. All through it I have come to discover that friendship is a real discipline. Nothing can be taken for granted, nothing happens automatically, nothing comes without concentrated effort. Friendship requires trust, patience, attentiveness, courage, repentance, forgiveness, celebration, and most of all faithfulness. It is amazing for me to realize how often

I thought that it was all over, that both Nathan and Sue had betrayed me or dropped me, and how easily feelings of jealousy, resentment, anger, and depression came over me. It is even more amazing to see that we are still friends, yes, the best of friends. But it certainly has been hard work for all three of us....

In this respect, my struggle with prayer is not so different from my struggle with friendship. Both prayer and friendship need purification. They need to become less dependent on fleeting emotions and more rooted in lasting commitments. As I write this, it sounds very wise! But I know already that my body and soul might need an immense amount of discipline to catch up with this wisdom.

After our dinner together, Sue, Nathan, and I saw the movie *Apollo 13*, about an aborted moon flight and the successful attempt to bring the three astronauts safely back to earth. Underneath all the spectacular technology there is the story of human relationships and the discipline required to make them lifesaving. As the three of us watched it, I realized that somehow we too are astronauts in a spaceship trying to make it home safely. I guess that is true of all people who take the risk of friendship.

—*Sabbatical Journey,* 7

Let others enlarge your perspective

Jonas and I had a lovely lunch at Harvard Square with Laurent, and we talked about Laurent's forthcoming book on commitment and worldwide compassion.... It is an impressive study based on many interviews and much research. One finding is that all people committed to large humanitarian causes at some point had a significant encounter with someone outside their own circles who was able to widen the boundaries of their lives and show them larger perspectives. Laurent said, "Underneath all the great commitments, you always find a significant relationship with someone who is truly 'other.'" I found that very insightful. And it confirmed my own experience. Without meeting Jean Vanier I would never have moved from Harvard to L'Arche. My commitment to live and work with handicapped people is indeed based on a relationship with someone who broke through my boundaries and radically enlarged my perspective. —*Sabbatical Journey*, 69

Love makes us feel alive

These days I feel strong, alive, and full of energy. Still, I am aware that much of that well-being is the direct result of the loving support of many friends. At the moment I do not experience any anger or hostility directed toward me. I feel in gentle harmony with my family, the people in Daybreak, especially Nathan and Sue, and the many friends close by and far away. In situations like this I easily forget how fragile I am inside, and how little is needed to throw me off balance. A small rejection, a slight criticism might be enough to make me doubt my self-worth and even lose my self-confidence.

I had been thinking about this when I read Michelangelo's poems to Tommaso Cavalieri, the young Roman nobleman whom he first met in 1532, when he was fifty-seven years old. His love for Tommaso, and Tommaso's affection for him, made him feel fully alive. He writes: "With your bright eyes, I see the living light which my blind eyes alone can never see; and your sure feet take up that load for me which my lame gait would let fall helplessly. My very thoughts are framed within your heart."

These words evoke deep feelings in me. They reveal my true dependence on human affection and love. I know how many of my thoughts are framed in the hearts of those who love me.

—*Sabbatical Journey,* 131–32

The way of the visitation

Today is the Feast of the Visitation. A very young girl meets a very old woman. Both are pregnant. Both feel misunderstood. Joseph, the young girl's fiancé, is considering separation, fearing scandal. Zechariah, the old woman's husband, has been struck dumb and doesn't understand what's happening. And the women themselves, do they know? Hardly. They are puzzled, confused, and somewhat lost.

Mary, the young girl, needs to get out of the little gossiping town where she lives. She suffers from staring eyes and whispers behind her back. She escapes. In haste she goes over the hills to Ain Karim, where her old cousin Elizabeth lives. She knows deep within her that Elizabeth will understand and offer her a safe place to wait for the child.

As they meet and look at each other, they shout with joy. They embrace, they hold each other, they cry, they laugh. The fear and self-consciousness fall away from both of them.

"The mother of my Lord," cries Elizabeth. "My soul magnifies the Lord," cries Mary. Elizabeth understands, affirms, and celebrates. Her whole body is jubilant. The child in her womb leaps with joy. And Mary realizes her grace, her gift, her special blessing.

With a newfound freedom she exclaims, "The Lord has looked with favor on the lowliness of this servant. Surely, from now on all generations will call me blessed, for the Mighty One has done great things for me" (Luke 1:43, 46–49).

Two women who felt oppressed and isolated suddenly realize their greatness and are free to celebrate their blessing. The two of them become community. They need each other, just to be together and protect each other, support each other, and affirm each other. They stay together for three months. Then each of them is ready to face her truth alone, without fear, willing to suffer the consequences of her motherhood.

I can hardly think about a better way to understand friendship, care, and love than "the way of the visitation." In a world so full of shame and guilt, we need to visit each other and offer each other a safe place where we can claim our freedom and celebrate our gifts. We need to get away once in a while from the suspicious voices and angry looks and be in a place where we are deeply understood and loved. Then we might be able to face the hostile world again, without fear and with new trust in our integrity.   —*Sabbatical Journey*, 175–76

Recognize your brother or sister

The rabbi asked his students: "How can we determine the hour of dawn, when the night ends and the day begins?"

One of the rabbi's students suggested: "When from a distance you can distinguish between a dog and a sheep?"

"No," was the answer of the rabbi.

"Is it when one can distinguish between a fig tree and a grapevine?" asked a second student.

"No," the rabbi said.

"Please tell us the answer, then," said the students.

"It is, then," said the wise teacher, "when you can look into the face of another human being and you have enough light in you to recognize your brother or your sister. Until then it is night, and darkness is still with us."

Let us pray for the light. It is the peace the world cannot give. —*Finding My Way Home*, 85–87

Befriend your weakness

One very important way to befriend our sorrow is to take it out of its isolation and share it with someone who can receive it. So much of our pain remains hidden — even from our closest friends. When we feel lonely, do we go to someone we trust and say: "I am lonely. I need your support and company." When we feel anxious, sexually needy, angry, or bitter, do we dare to ask a friend to be with us and receive our pain.

Too often we think or say: "I don't want to bother my friends with my problems. They have enough problems themselves." But the truth is that we honor our friends by entrusting our struggles to them. Don't we ourselves say to our friends who have hidden their feelings of fear and shame from us: "Why didn't you tell me, why did you keep it secret so long?" Obviously, not everyone can receive our hidden pains. But I believe that if we truly desire to grow in spiritual maturity, God will send us the friends we need.

So much of our suffering arises not just out of our painful condition, but from our feeling of isolation in the midst of our pain. Many people who suffer immensely from addiction—be it addiction to alcohol, drugs, sex, or food—find their first real relief when they can share their pain with others and discover that they are truly heard. The many twelve-step programs are a powerful witness to the truth that sharing our pain is the beginning of healing. Here we can see how close sorrow and joy can be. When I discover that I am no longer alone in my struggle and when I start experiencing a new "fellowship in weakness," then true joy can erupt, right in the middle of my sorrow.

But it is not easy to step out of our isolation. Somehow we always want to solve our problems on our own. But God has given us to each other to build a community of mutual love where we can discover together that joy is not just for others but for all of us.

—*Here and Now*, 40–42

Move beyond individualism

Much of our isolation is self-chosen. We do not like to be dependent on others and, whenever possible, we try to show ourselves that we are in control of the situation and can make our own decisions. This self-reliance has many attractions. It gives us a sense of power, it allows us to move quickly, it offers us the satisfaction of being our own boss, and it promises many rewards and prizes.

However, the underside of this self-reliance is loneliness, isolation, and a constant fear of not making it in life.

I have experienced the rewards as well as the punishments of individualism. As a university professor, I was a productive and popular teacher and made it through the many hoops of academic promotion, but at the very end of it all, I felt quite alone. Notwithstanding all the praise I was receiving while speaking about community, I didn't feel that I truly belonged to anyone. While showing convincingly the importance of prayer, I myself lost the ability to be quiet enough to pray. While encouraging mutual vulnerability as a way to grow in the Spirit, I found myself quite careful and even defensive where my own reputation was at stake. The bottom line for academics is competition — even for those who preach compassion — at least when they don't want to lose their jobs!

To make compassion the bottom line of life, to be open and vulnerable to others, to make community life the focus, and to let prayer be the breath of your life...that requires a willingness to tear down the countless walls that we have erected between ourselves and others in order to maintain our safe isolation. This is a lifelong and arduous spiritual battle because while tearing down walls with one hand, we build new ones with the other. After I had left the university and chosen a life in community, I realized that, even in community, there are numerous ways to play the controlling games of individualism. Indeed, true conversion asks for a lot more than a change of place. It asks for a change of heart.

—*Here and Now*, 42–43

Our desire for communion

What do we really desire? As I try to listen to my own deepest yearning as well as to the yearnings of others, the word that seems best to summarize the desire of the human heart is "communion." Communion means "union with." God has given us a heart that will remain restless until it has found full communion. We look for it in friendship, in marriage, in community. We look for it in sexual intimacy, in moments of ecstasy, in the recognition of our gifts. We look for it through success, admiration, and rewards. But wherever we look, it is communion that we seek.

As I looked at the faces of the gold medalists at the Olympics, with more than sixty thousand people applauding them and millions watching them on television, I caught a glimpse of that momentary experience of communion. It seemed as if they had, finally, received the love they had worked for with unwavering dedication. And still, how soon they will be forgotten. Four, eight, or twelve years later, others will take their place on the platform of success, and their brief moment of glory will be remembered by very few.

Still, the desire for communion remains. It is a God-given desire, a desire that causes immense pain as well as immense joy. Jesus came to proclaim that our desire for communion is not in vain, but will be fulfilled by the One who gave us that desire. The passing moments of communion are only hints of the Communion that God has promised us. The real danger facing us is to distrust our desire for communion. It is a God-given desire without which our lives lose their vitality and our hearts grow cold. A truly spiritual life is life in which we won't rest until we have found rest in the embrace of the One who is the Father and Mother of all desires.

—*Here and Now*, 43–44

Choose a spiritual milieu

We cannot live a spiritual life alone. The life of the Spirit is like a seed that needs fertile ground to grow. This fertile ground includes not only a good inner disposition, but also a supportive milieu.

It is very hard to live a life of prayer in a milieu where no one prays or speaks lovingly about prayer. It is nearly impossible to deepen our communion with God when those with whom we live and work reject or even ridicule the idea that there is a loving God. It is a superhuman task to keep setting our hearts on the kingdom when all those whom we know and talk with are setting their hearts on everything but the kingdom.

It is not surprising that people who live in a secular milieu—where God's name is never mentioned, prayer unknown, the Bible never read, and conversation about the life in the Spirit completely absent—cannot sustain their communion with God for very long. I have discovered how sensitive I am to the milieu in which I live. With my community, words about God's presence in our life come spontaneously and with great ease. However, when I join in a business meeting in downtown Toronto or keep company with those who work with AIDS patients, a conversation about God often creates embarrassment or even anger and generally ends up in a debate about the pros and cons of religion that leaves everybody unhappy.

When we are serious about living a spiritual life we are responsible for the milieu where it can grow and mature. Although we might not be able to create the ideal context for a life in the Spirit, we have many more options than we often claim for ourselves. We can choose friends, books, churches, art, music, places to visit, and people to be with that, taken together, offer a milieu that allows the mustard seed that God has sown in us to grow into a strong tree.   —*Here and Now, 95–96*

Free to follow Jesus

Leaving father, mother, brothers, and sisters for Jesus' sake is a lifelong task. It is only gradually that we realize how we go on clinging to the negative as well as to the positive experiences of our youth and how hard it is to leave it all and be on our own. To leave "home," whether it was a good or a bad home, is one of the greatest spiritual challenges of our life.

I had already left my family and my country for more than twenty years when I became fully aware that I was still trying to live up to the expectations of my father and mother. In fact, I was shocked when I found out that many of my work habits, career decisions, and life choices were still deeply motivated by my desire to please my family. I still wanted to be the son or the brother they could be proud of.

74

When I saw this in myself, I also started to see it in the lives of many of my friends. Some of them, who already had grown-up children, still suffered from the rejection they experienced from their parents. Others who carved out impressive careers and won many rewards and prizes still had deep hopes that, one day, their father or mother would acknowledge their gifts. Others again, who suffered many disappointments in their personal relations or work, still blamed their parents for their misfortunes.

The older we grow, the more we come to see the deep roots of our ties with those who were our main guides during the formative years of our lives.

Jesus wants to set us free, free from everything that prevents us from fully following our vocation, free also from everyone who prevents us from fully knowing God's unconditional love. To come to that freedom we have to keep leaving our fathers, mothers, brothers, and sisters, and dare to follow him...even there where we rather would not go.

—Here and Now, 113–14

Choose your friends

The spiritual life is one of constant choices. One of the most important choices is the choice of the people with whom we develop close intimate relationships. We have only a limited amount of time in our lives. With whom do we spend it and how? That's probably one of the most decisive questions of our lives. It is not without reason that parents are very concerned about who their children bring home as playmates, friends, or lovers. They know that much of their children's happiness will depend on those they choose to be close to.

To whom do we go for advice? With whom do we spend our free evenings? With whom are we going on vacation? Sometimes we speak or act as if we have little choice in the matter. Sometimes we act as though we will be lucky if there is anyone who wants to be our friend. But that is a very passive and even fatalistic attitude. If we truly believe that God loves us with an unlimited, unconditional love, then we can trust that there are women and men in this world who are eager to show us that love. But we cannot wait passively until someone shows up to offer us friendship. As people who trust in God's love, we must have the courage and the confidence to say to someone through whom God's love becomes visible to us: "I would like to get to know you, I would like to spend time with you. I would like to develop a friendship with you. What about you?"

There will be no's, there will be the pain of rejection. But when we determine to avoid all no's and all rejections, we will never create the milieu where we can grow stronger and deepen in love. God became human for us to make divine love tangible. That is what incarnation is all about. That incarnation not only happened long ago, but it continues to happen for those who trust that God will give us the friends we need. But the choice is ours!

—Here and Now, 131–32

GIVE THANKS

Third, you have to celebrate your chosenness constantly. This means saying "thank you" to God for having chosen you, and "thank you" to all who remind you of your chosenness.   *—Life of the Beloved,* 50

Belong and bless

In one of Jesus' stories a Pharisee, standing by himself, prays to God: "God, I thank you that I am not like other people" (Luke 18:11).

That's a prayer we often pray. "I'm glad I'm not like him, her, or them. I am lucky not to belong to that family, that country, or that race. I am blessed not to be part of that company, that team, or that crowd!" Most of this prayer is unceasing! Somewhere we are always comparing ourselves with others, trying to convince ourselves that we are better off than they are. It is a prayer that wells up from our fearful selves and guides many of our thoughts and actions.

But this is a very dangerous prayer. It leads from compassion to competition, from competition to rivalry, from rivalry to violence, from violence to war, from war to destruction. It is a prayer that lies all the time, because we are not the difference we try so hard to find. No, our deepest identity is rooted where we are like other people — weak, broken, sinful, but sons and daughters of God.

I even think that we should not thank God for not being like other creatures, animals, plants, or rocks! We should thank God that indeed we are like them, not better or worse but integral parts of God's creation. This is what humility is all about. We belong to the humus, the soil, and it is in this belonging that we can find the deepest reason for gratitude. Our prayer must be, "Thank you, God, that I am worthy to be part of your creation. Be merciful to me a sinner."

Through this prayer we will be justified (see Luke 18:14), that is, find our just place in God's Kingdom.

—*Sabbatical Journey,* 128

The choice of the heart

It might sound strange to say that joy is the result of our choices. We often imagine that some people are luckier than others and that their joy or sorrow depends on the circumstances of their life—over which they have no control.

However, we do have a choice, not so much in regard to the circumstances of our life, but in regard to the way we respond to these circumstances. Two people can be the victims of the same accident. For the one, it becomes the source of resentment; for the other, the source of gratitude. The external circumstances are the same, but the choice of response is completely different. Some people become bitter as they grow old. Others grow old joyfully. That does not mean that the life of those who become bitter was harder than the life of those who become joyful. It means that different choices were made, inner choices, choices of the heart.

It is important to become aware that at every moment of our life we have an opportunity to choose joy. Life has many sides to it. There are always sorrowful and joyful sides to the reality we live. And so we always have a choice to live the moment as a cause for resentment or as a cause for joy. It is in the choice that our true freedom lies, and that freedom is, in the final analysis, the freedom to love.

It might be a good idea to ask ourselves how we develop our capacity to choose for joy. Maybe we could spend a moment at the end of each day and decide to remember that day — whatever may have happened — as a day to be grateful for. In so doing we increase our heart's capacity to choose for joy. And as our hearts become more joyful, we will become, without any special effort, a source of joy for others. Just as sadness begets sadness, so joy begets joy.

—Here and Now, 27–28

Be a spiritual realist

Joy is contagious, just as sorrow is. I have a friend who radiates joy, not because his life is easy, but because he habitually recognizes God's presence in the midst of all human suffering, his own as well as others'. Wherever he goes, whomever he meets, he is able to see and hear something beautiful, something for which to be grateful. He doesn't deny the great sorrow that surrounds him nor is he blind or deaf to the agonizing sights and sounds of his fellow human beings, but his spirit gravitates toward the light in the darkness and the prayers in the midst of the cries of despair. His eyes are gentle; his voice is soft. There is nothing sentimental about him. He is a realist, but his deep faith allows him to know that hope is more real than despair, faith more real than distrust, and love more real than fear. It is this spiritual realism that makes him such a joyful man.

Whenever I meet him, I am tempted to draw his attention to the wars between nations, the starvation among children, the corruption in politics, and the deceit among people, thus trying to impress him with the ultimate brokenness of the human race. But every time I try something like this, he looks at me with his gentle and compassionate eyes and says: "I saw two children sharing their bread with one another, and I heard a woman say 'thank you' and smile when someone covered her with a blanket. These simple poor people gave me new courage to live my life."

My friend's joy is contagious. The more I am with him, the more I catch glimpses of the sun shining through the clouds. Yes, I know there is a sun, even though the skies are covered with clouds. While my friend always spoke about the sun, I kept speaking about the clouds, until one day I realized that it was the sun that allowed me to see the clouds.

Those who keep speaking about the sun while walking under a cloudy sky are messengers of hope, the true saints of our day.   —*Here and Now,* 28–29

Be surprised by joy

Are we surprised by joy or by sorrow? The world in which we live wants to surprise us by sorrow. Newspapers keep telling us about traffic accidents, murders, conflicts between individuals, groups, and nations, and the television fills our minds with images of hatred, violence, and destruction. And we say to one another: "Did you hear that, did you see that...isn't it terrible...who can believe it?" Indeed it seems that the powers of darkness want to continue to surprise us with human sorrow. But these surprises paralyze us and seduce us to an existence in which our main concern becomes survival in the midst of a sea of sorrows. By making us think about ourselves as survivors of a shipwreck, anxiously clinging to a piece of driftwood, we gradually accept the role of victims doomed by the cruel circumstances of our lives.

The great challenge of faith is to be surprised by joy. I remember sitting at a dinner table with friends discussing the economic depression of the country. We kept throwing out statistics that made us increasingly convinced that things could only get worse. Then, suddenly, the four-year-old son of one of my friends opened the door, ran to his father, and said, "Look, Daddy! Look! I found a little kitten in the yard . . . Look! . . . Isn't she cute?" While showing the kitten to his father, the little boy stroked the kitten with his hands and held it against his face. All at once everything changed. The little boy and his kitten became the center of attention. There were smiles, strokes, and many tender words. We were surprised by joy!

God became a little child in the midst of a violent world. Are we surprised by joy or do we keep saying: "How nice and sweet, but the reality is different." What if the child reveals to us what is really real?

—Here and Now, 29–30

Remember with gratitude

How can we live a truly grateful life? When we look back at all that has happened to us, we easily divide our lives into good things to be grateful for and bad things to forget. But with a past thus divided, we cannot move freely into the future. With many things to forget we can only limp toward the future.

True spiritual gratitude embraces all of our past, the good as well as the bad events, the joyful as well as the sorrowful moments. From the place where we stand, everything that took place brought us to this place, and we want to remember all of it as part of God's guidance. That does not mean that all that happened in the past was good, but it does mean that even the bad didn't happen outside the loving presence of God.

Jesus' own suffering was brought upon him by the forces of darkness. Still he speaks about his suffering and death as his way to glory.

It is very hard to keep bringing all of our past under the light of gratitude. There are so many things about which we feel guilt and shame, so many things we simply wish had never happened. But each time we have the courage to look at "the all of it" and to look at it as God looks at it, our guilt becomes a happy guilt and our shame a happy shame because they have brought us to a deeper recognition of God's mercy, a stronger conviction of God's guidance, and a more radical commitment to a life in God's service.

Once all of our past is remembered in gratitude, we are free to be sent into the world to proclaim good news to others. Just as Peter's denials didn't paralyze him but, once forgiven, became a new source of his faithfulness, so can all our failures and betrayals be transformed into gratitude and enable us to become messengers of hope. —*Here and Now*, 81–82

Give and receive

One of the most beautiful characteristics of the compassionate life is that there is always a mutuality of giving and receiving. Everyone who has truly entered into the compassionate life will say: "I have received as much as I have given." Those who have worked with the dying in Calcutta, those who have lived among the poor in the "young towns" of Lima or the "favelas" of São Paulo, those who have dedicated themselves to AIDS patients or mentally handicapped people—they all will express deep gratitude for the gifts received from those they came to help. There is probably no clearer sign of true compassion than this mutuality of giving and receiving.

One of the most memorable times of my own life was the time I spent living with the Osco Moreno family in Pamplona Alta near Lima, Peru. Pablo and his wife,

Sophia, with their three children, Johnny, Maria, and Pablito, offered me their generous hospitality, even though they were very poor. I will never forget their smiles, their affection, their playfulness — all of that in the midst of a life full of worries about how to make it for another day. I went to Peru with a deep desire to help the poor. I returned home with a deep gratitude for what I had received. Later, while teaching at Harvard Divinity School, I often felt a real homesickness for "my family." I missed the children hanging onto my arms and legs, laughing loudly and sharing their cookies and drinks with me. I missed the spontaneity, the intimacy, and the generosity with which the poor of Pamplona Alta surrounded me. They literally showered me with gifts of love. No doubt, they were happy and even proud to have this tall "Gringo Padre" with them, but whatever I gave them, it was nothing compared to what I received.

The rewards of compassion are not things to wait for. They are hidden in compassion itself. I know this for sure. —*Here and Now*, 107–8

Forgive and be grateful

Two of the most important ways of leaving father, mother, brother, and sister are forgiveness and gratitude. Can we forgive our family for not having loved us as well as we wanted to be loved? Can we forgive our fathers for being demanding, authoritarian, indifferent, unaffectionate, absent, or simply more interested in other people or things than in us? Can we forgive our mothers for being possessive, scrupulous, controlling, preoccupied, addicted to food, alcohol, or drugs, overly busy, or simply more concerned with a career than with us? Can we forgive our brothers and sisters for not playing with us, for not sharing their friends with us, for talking down to us, or for making us feel stupid or useless?

There is a lot to forgive, not just because our family was not as caring as other families, but because all the love we received was imperfect and very limited. Our parents also are children of parents who didn't love them in a perfect way, and even our grandparents had parents who were not ideal!

There is so much to forgive. But if we are willing to see our own parents, grandparents, and great-grandparents as people like ourselves with a desire to love but also with many unfulfilled needs, we might be able to step over our anger, our resentments, or even our hatred, and discover that their limited love is still real love, a love for which to be grateful.

Once we are able to forgive, we can be grateful for what we have received. And we have received so much. We can walk, talk, smile, move, laugh, cry, eat, drink, dance, play, work, sing, give life, give joy, give hope, give love. We are alive! Our fathers and mothers gave us life, and our brothers and sisters helped us to live it. Once we are no longer blinded by their so obvious weaknesses, we can see clearly how much there is to be grateful for.

—*Here and Now,* 114–15

Bless

Let me first tell you what I mean by the word "blessing." In Latin, to bless is *benedicere*. The word "benediction" that is used in many churches means literally: speaking (*dictio*) well (*bene*) or saying good things of someone.... To give someone a blessing is the most significant affirmation we can offer. It is more than a word of praise or appreciation; it is more than pointing out someone's talents or good deeds; it is more than putting someone in the light. To give a blessing is to affirm, to say "yes" to a person's Belovedness.

—*Life of the Beloved*, 56–57

The very idea of giving or receiving a blessing presumes a relationship. Henri reminds us that to bless another (or to be blessed by someone) is to "speak well of others —

to say 'yes' to another's being." Learning to affirm and celebrate another's worth, beauty, and uniqueness as a beloved child of God was one of Henri Nouwen's recurring themes.

Henri learned through many friendships that community is another means of experiencing God's blessing. He had a remarkable ability to cut to the core of meaning in conversations and loved to celebrate the moment with good food and laughter. He loved deeply and knew first-hand that those closest to us can bless or curse, but when they bless us, the wonder of God's approval is conveyed through human hands.

In 1985 Henri spent a week at Daybreak while in Toronto on other business. During this time one of the core members, Raymond, was involved in a serious car accident. Despite his status as a visitor, Henri stepped right into the crisis as the resident priest. He visited the hospital and established a relationship with the distraught family. He visited various homes in the Daybreak community where assistants live with core members—those with mental disabilities—and encouraged each household to place a photo of Raymond on their dining room tables to remind them to pray for him. At the hospital, Henri encouraged Raymond's father to bless his son and say the things in his heart should his son die before there was another opportunity. Raymond's father protested that he did not know how to offer such a blessing. Henri said, "I'll show you. Bless your son and say good things to him. Tell him that you love him and speak to him about God." He enacted for many what it meant to say "yes" to others.

Henri's family affirmed that he expressed a desire to become a priest at six years of age. As the firstborn son of a devout Catholic family and the nephew of a well-known Dutch priest, his vocation as a priest was recognized early and encouraged. By the age of eight he had converted the attic into a chapel where he said Mass. His mother and grandmother commissioned a carpenter to build a tiny altar and a seamstress to sew child-sized vestments for her sensitive and outgoing son. These actions weren't unusual in Henri's Dutch Catholic community, but the vigor of Henri's role playing was noteworthy.

To Henri, this childhood church play was not a game to outgrow. He sensed he was marked by God for a special purpose. His calling was a blessing that would bring him joy and fame, sorrow and despair. In Latin to be a priest literally means to be a bridge builder between the human and divine.

When Henri was ordained in Utrecht in The Netherlands on July 21, 1957, his uncle gifted him with his handcrafted gold chalice adorned with Henri's maternal grandmother's diamonds. He loved the family chalice and used it when he first celebrated Mass the next morning. As was the Catholic practice, pre-Vatican II, he distributed the bread and alone drank from the cup, experiencing a deep sense of unity with Jesus. Later in life, Henri came to prefer a large glass chalice that could be shared with others. The transparency and simplicity of these cups, Henri wrote, "speak about a new way of being a priest and a new way of being human."

Whenever Henri traveled—and it was often—he continued his daily practice of celebrating the Eucharist wherever he was, either alone or with any group he could spontaneously gather. Anyone who ever saw him raise a glass chalice with his elegant hands would have seen the caressing touch with which he performed his sacred task. He loved the feel of the chalice, the earthy, full taste of the wine, and the great sacrifice of love it reenacted. When he offered it; there was no doubt that this was a cup of blessing.

In Can You Drink the Cup? Henri tells the story of visiting another of Daybreak's core members, Trevor, who was undergoing an evaluation in a mental hospital. Upon learning that the famous priest was going to visit, the hospital chaplain had invited some area clergy and hospital staff to a luncheon. Henri arrived and was welcomed warmly and taken to the lovely dining room. When Henri asked for Trevor, he was told that it was against hospital protocol for staff and patients to eat together in the Golden Room reserved for special occasions.

Henri, the bridge-builder priest, refused to dine without Trevor. So Trevor was allowed to join the group. While most seated at the tables engaged in polite conversation, Trevor stood, lifted his Coke, and said: "Lift up your glasses." Most did, and then Trevor unabashedly began to sing, "When you're happy and you know it, lift your glass...." Henri writes, "Trevor's toast radically changed the mood in the Golden Room. He had brought these strangers together and made them feel at home. His beautiful smile and his fearless joy had broken down the barriers between staff and patients and created a happy family of caring people. With his unique blessing, Trevor had set the tone for a joyful and fruitful meeting. The cup of sorrow and joy had become the cup of blessings."

This second collection of pearls from Henri's books focuses on the what it means to bless. The first group, "Listen in Prayer," centers on the inner life, where prayerful listening must be cultivated. The second group, "Cultivate Presence," encourages awareness and attentiveness to the moments in each day that affirm and celebrate the truth that each day carries blessings, if we take time to look and see, taste and enjoy.

As you read, these selections may trigger memories of friends and special moments in your own life. Savor them. Here's a suggestion: Read with a sheet of paper at hand. Stop between selections and list the blessings that come *to your mind as you read. Simply place one right after the other—short phrases, names, memories, graces, kind words, difficult times soldiered through, and insights. Be attentive to the blessings that come to you day after day, year after year. Look to your heart, listen to God's voice of love, and heed the small and large moments of goodness in your own life. It's true. You are being blessed.*

—R.L.

LISTEN IN PRAYER

Let me offer you two suggestions for claiming your blessedness. These have to do with prayer and presence. First of all, prayer. For me personally, prayer becomes more and more a way to listen to the blessing. I have read and written much about prayer, but when I go to a quiet place to pray, I realize that, although I have a tendency to say many things to God, the real "work" of prayer is to become silent and listen to the voice that says good things about me. This might sound self-indulgent, but, in practice, it is a hard discipline. —*Life of the Beloved*, 62

Let the Spirit blow freely

Prayer is the bridge between my unconscious and conscious life. Prayer connects my mind with my heart, my will with my passions, my brain with my belly. Prayer is the way to let the life-giving Spirit of God penetrate all the corners of my being. Prayer is the divine instrument of my wholeness, unity, and inner peace.

So, what about my life of prayer? Do I like to pray? Do I want to pray? Do I spend time praying? Frankly, the answer is no to all three questions. After sixty-three years of life and thirty-eight years of priesthood, my prayer seems as dead as a rock. I remember fondly my teenage years, when I could hardly stay away from the church. For hours I would stay on my knees filled with a deep sense of Jesus' presence. I couldn't believe that not everyone wanted to pray. Prayer was so intimate and so satisfying. It was during these prayer-filled years that my vocation to the priesthood was shaped. During the years that followed I have paid much attention to prayer, reading about it, writing about it, visiting monasteries and houses of prayer, and guiding many people on their spiritual journeys. By now I should be full of spiritual fire, consumed by prayer. Many people think I am and speak to me as if prayer is my greatest gift and deepest desire.

The truth is that I do not feel much, if anything, when I pray. There are no warm emotions, bodily sensations, or mental visions. None of my five senses is being touched—no special smells, no special sounds, no special sights, no special tastes, and no special movements. Whereas for a long time the Spirit acted so clearly through my flesh, now I feel nothing. I have lived with the expectation that prayer would become easier as I grow older and closer to death. But the opposite seems to be happening. The words "darkness" and "dryness" seem to best describe my prayer today.

Maybe part of this darkness and dryness is the result of my overactivity. As I grow older I become busier and spend less and less time in prayer. But I probably should not blame myself in that way. The real questions are, "What are the darkness and the dryness about? What do they call me to?" . . .

Are the darkness and dryness of my prayer signs of God's absence, or are they signs of a presence deeper and wider than my senses can contain? Is the death of my prayer the end of my intimacy with God or the beginning of a new communion, beyond words, emotions, and bodily sensations? . . .

Maybe the time has come to let go of *my* prayer, *my* effort to be close to God, *my* way of being in communion with the Divine, and to allow the Spirit of God to blow freely in me. Paul writes, "What you received was not the spirit of slavery to bring you back into fear; you received the spirit of adoption, enabling us to cry out, 'Abba, Father!' The living Spirit joins with our spirit to bear witness that we are children of God" (Rom. 8:14–16).   —*Sabbatical Journey, 5*

Life in the present

To live in the present, we must believe deeply that what is most important is the here and the now. We are constantly distracted by things that have happened in the past or that might happen in the future. It is not easy to remain focused on the present. Our mind is hard to master and keeps pulling us away from the moment.

Prayer is the discipline of the moment. When we pray, we enter into the presence of God whose name is God-with-us. To pray is to listen attentively to the One who addresses us here and now. When we dare to trust that we are never alone but that God is always with us, always cares for us, and always speaks to us, then we can gradually detach ourselves from the voices that make us guilty or anxious and thus allow ourselves to dwell in the present moment. This is a very hard challenge because radical trust in God is not obvious. Most of us distrust God. Most of us think of God as a fearful, punitive authority or as an empty, powerless nothing. Jesus' core message was that God is neither a powerless weakling nor a powerful boss, but a lover, whose only desire is to give us what our hearts most desire.

To pray is to listen to that voice of love. That is what obedience is all about. The word "obedience" comes from the Latin word *ob-audire,* which means to listen with great attentiveness. Without listening, we become "deaf" to the voice of love. The Latin word for deaf is *surdus.* To be completely deaf is to be *absurdus,* yes, absurd. When we no longer pray, no longer listen to the voice of love that speaks to us in the moment, our lives become absurd lives in which we are thrown back and forth between the past and the future.

If we could just be, for a few minutes each day, fully where we are, we would indeed discover that we are not alone and that the One who is with us wants only one thing: to give us love.   —*Here and Now,* 19–20

Our inner room

Listening to the voice of love requires that we direct our minds and hearts toward that voice with all our attention. How can we do that? The most fruitful way—in my experience—is to take a simple prayer, a sentence or a word, and slowly repeat it. We can use the Lord's Prayer, the Jesus Prayer, the name of Jesus, or any word that reminds us of God's love and put it in the center of our inner room, like a candle in a dark space.

Obviously we will be constantly distracted. We will think about what happened yesterday or what will happen tomorrow. We will have long, imaginary discussions with our friends or enemies. We will plan our next day, prepare our upcoming talk, or organize our next meeting. Still, as long as we keep the candle in our dark room burning, we can return to that light and see clearly the presence of the One who offers us what we most desire.

This is not always a satisfying experience. Often we are so restless and so unable to find inner quietude that we can't wait to get busy again, thus avoiding the confrontation with the chaotic state of our minds and hearts. Still, when we remain faithful to our discipline, even if it is only ten minutes a day, we gradually come to see—by the candlelight of our prayers—that there is a space within us where God dwells and where we are invited to dwell with God. Once we come to know that inner, holy place, a place more beautiful and precious than any place we can travel to, we want to be there and be spiritually fed.

—*Here and Now,* 21

Pray for one another

One of the discoveries we make in prayer is that the closer we come to God, the closer we come to all our brothers and sisters in the human family. God is not a private God. The God who dwells in our inner sanctuary is also the God who dwells in the inner sanctuary of each human being. As we recognize God's presence in our own hearts, we can also recognize that presence in the hearts of others, because the God who has chosen us as a dwelling-place gives us the eyes to see the God who dwells in others. When we see only demons within ourselves, we can see only demons in others, but when we see God within ourselves, we can see God also in others.

This might sound rather theoretical, but when we pray, we will increasingly experience ourselves as part of a human family infinitely bound by God, who created us to share, all of us, in the divine light.

We often wonder what we can do for others, especially for those in great need. It is not a sign of powerlessness when we say: "We must pray for one another." To pray for one another is, first of all, to acknowledge, in the presence of God, that we belong to each other as children of the same God. Without this acknowledgment of human solidarity, what we do for one another does not flow from who we truly are. We are brothers and sisters, not competitors or rivals. We are children of one God, not partisans of different gods.

To pray, that is, to listen to the voice of the One who calls us the "beloved," is to learn that that voice excludes no one. Where I dwell, God dwells with me and where God dwells with me I find all my sisters and brothers. And so intimacy with God and solidarity with all people are two aspects of dwelling in the present moment that can never be separated.

—*Here and Now,* 22–23

The hub of life

In my home country, the Netherlands, you still see many large wagon wheels, not on wagons, but as decorations at the entrances of farms or on the walls of restaurants. I have always been fascinated by these wagon wheels: with their wide rims, strong wooden spokes, and big hubs. These wheels help me to understand the importance of a life lived from the center. When I move along the rim, I can reach one spoke after the other, but when I stay at the hub, I am in touch with all the spokes at once.

To pray is to move to the center of all life and all love. The closer I come to the hub of life, the closer I come to all that receives its strength and energy from there. My tendency is to get so distracted by the diversity of the many spokes of life that I am busy but not truly life-giving, all over the place but not focused. By directing my attention to the heart of life, I am connected with its rich variety while remaining centered. What does the hub represent? I think of it as my own heart, the heart of God, and the heart of the world. When I pray, I enter into the depth of my own heart and find there the heart of God, who speaks to me of love. And I recognize, right there, the place where all of my sisters and brothers are in communion with one another. The great paradox of the spiritual life is, indeed, that the most personal is most universal, that the most intimate, is most communal, and that the most contemplative is most active.

The wagon wheel shows that the hub is the center of all energy and movement, even when it often seems not to be moving at all. In God all action and all rest are one. So too prayer! —*Here and Now*, 23–24

A clear goal

Do we have a clear goal in life? The athletes whose clear goal is the attainment of the Olympic gold are willing to let everything else become secondary. The way they eat, sleep, study, and train are all determined by that one clear goal.

This is as true in the spiritual life as it is in the life of competitive sports. Without a clear goal, we will always be distracted and spend our energy on secondary things. "Keep your eye on the prize," Martin Luther King said to his people. What is our prize? Is it the divine life, the eternal life, the life with and in God. Jesus proclaimed to us that goal, that heavenly prize. To Nicodemus he said: "This is how God loved the world: he gave his Son so that everyone who believes in him may not perish but may have eternal life" (John 3:16).

It is not easy to keep our eyes fixed on the eternal life, especially not in a world that keeps telling us that there are more immediate and urgent things on which to focus. There is scarcely a day that does not pull our attention away from our goal and make it look vague and cloudy. But still, we know from experience that without a clear goal our lives become fragmented into many tasks and obligations that drain us and leave us with a feeling of exhaustion and uselessness. How then do we keep our goal clear, how then do we fix our eyes on the prize? By the discipline of prayer: the discipline that helps us to bring God back again and again to the center of our life. We will always remain distracted, constantly busy with many urgent demands, but when there is a time and place set apart to return to our God who offers us eternal life, we gradually can come to realize that the many things we have to do, to say, or to think no longer distract us but are, instead, all leading us closer to our goal. Important, however, is that our goal remains clear. Prayer keeps our goal clear, and when our goal has become vague, prayer makes it clear again.   —*Here and Now*, 68–69

The still small voice

Recently I was standing at the corner of Bloor and Yonge streets in downtown Toronto. I saw a young man crossing the street while the stoplight turned red. He just missed being hit by a car. Meanwhile, hundreds of people were moving in all directions. Most faces looked quite tense and serious, and no one greeted anyone. They were all absorbed in their own thoughts, trying to reach some unknown goal. Long rows of cars and trucks were crossing the intersection or making right and left turns in the midst of the large pedestrian crowd.

I wondered: "What is going on in the minds of all these people. What are they trying to do, what are they hoping for, what is pushing them?" As I stood at that busy intersection, I wished I were able to overhear the inner ruminations of all these people. But I soon realized that I didn't have to be so curious. My own restlessness was probably not very different from that of all those around me!

Why is it so difficult to be still and quiet and let God speak to me about the meaning of my life. Is it because I don't trust God? Is it because I don't know God? Is it because I wonder if God really is there for me? Is it because I am afraid of God? Is it because everything else is more real for me than God? Is it because, deep down, I do not believe that God cares what happens at the corner of Yonge and Bloor?

Still there is a voice — right there, in downtown Toronto. "Come to me, you who labor and are over-burdened, and I will give you rest. Shoulder my yoke and learn from me, for I am gentle and humble in heart, and you will find rest for your soul. Yes, my yoke is easy and my burden light" (Matt. 11:28–30).

Can I trust that voice and follow it? It is not a very loud voice, and often it is drowned out by the clamor of the inner city. Still, when I listen attentively, I will hear that voice again and again and come to recognize it as the voice speaking to the deepest places of my heart.   —*Here and Now*, 76–77

Mother Teresa's answer

Once, quite a few years ago, I had the opportunity of meeting Mother Teresa of Calcutta. I was struggling with many things at the time and decided to use the occasion to ask Mother Teresa's advice. As soon as we sat down I started explaining all my problems and difficulties—trying to convince her of how complicated it all was! When, after ten minutes of elaborate explanation, I finally became silent, Mother

Teresa looked at me quietly and said: "Well, when you spend one hour a day adoring your Lord and never do anything which you know is wrong...you will be fine!"

When she said this I realized suddenly that she had punctured my big balloon of complex self-complaints and pointed me far beyond myself to the place of real healing. In fact, I was so stunned by her answer that I didn't feel any desire or need to continue the conversation. The many people waiting outside the room to see her could probably use her time better than I. So I thanked her and left. Her few words became engraved on my heart and mind and remain to this day. I had not expected these words, but in their directness and simplicity, they cut through to the center of my being. I knew that she had *spoken* the truth and that I had the rest of my life to *live* it.

Reflecting on this brief but decisive encounter, I realize that I had raised a question from below and that she had given an answer from above. At first, her answer didn't seem to fit my question, but then I began to see that her answer came from God's place and not from the place of my complaints. Most of the time we respond to questions from below with answers from below. The result is more questions and more answers and, often, more confusion.

Mother Teresa's answer was like a flash of lightning in my darkness. I suddenly knew the truth about myself. —*Here and Now*, 88–89

From worry to prayer

One of the least helpful ways to stop worrying is to try hard not to think about the things we are worrying about. We cannot push away our worries with our minds. When I lie in my bed worrying about an upcoming meeting, I can't stop my worries by saying to myself: "Don't think about these things; just fall asleep. Things will work out fine tomorrow." My mind simply answers: "How do you know?" and is back worrying again.

Jesus' advice to set our hearts on God's kingdom is somewhat paradoxical. You might give it the following interpretation: "If you want to worry, worry about that which is worth the effort. Worry about larger things than your family, your friends, or tomorrow's meeting. Worry about the things of God: truth, life, and light!"

As soon, however, as we set our hearts on these things our minds stop spinning because we enter into communion with the One who is present to us here and now and is there to give us what we most need.

108

And so worrying becomes prayer, and our feelings of powerlessness are transformed into a consciousness of being empowered by God's spirit.

Indeed, we cannot prolong our lives by worrying, but we can move far beyond the boundaries of our short life span and claim eternal life as God's beloved children.

Does that put an end to our worrying? Probably not. As long as we are in our world, full of tensions and pressures, our minds will never be free from worries, but when we keep returning with our hearts and minds to God's embracing love, we will be able to keep smiling at our own worrisome selves and keep our eyes and ears open for the sights and sounds of the kingdom. —*Here and Now*, 89–90

Move from mind to heart

How do we concretely go about setting our hearts on God's kingdom? When I lie in my bed, not able to fall asleep because of my many worries, when I do my work preoccupied about all the things that can go wrong, when I can't get my mind off my concern for a dying friend—what am I supposed to do? Set my heart on the kingdom? Fine, but how does one do this?

There are as many answers to this question as there are people with different lifestyles, personalities, and external circumstances. There is not one specific answer that fits everyone's needs. But there are some answers that can offer helpful directions.

One simple answer is to move from the mind to the heart by slowly saying a prayer with as much attentiveness as possible. This may sound like offering a crutch to someone who asks you to heal his broken leg. The truth, however, is that a prayer, prayed from the heart, heals. When you know the Our Father, the Apostles' Creed, the Glory Be to the Father by heart, you have something to start with. You might like to learn by heart the Twenty-third Psalm: "The Lord is my shepherd..." or Paul's words about love to the Corinthians or St. Francis's prayer: "Lord, make me an instrument of your peace...." As you lie in your bed, drive your car, wait for the bus, or walk your dog, you can slowly let the words of one of these prayers go through your mind simply trying to listen with your whole being to what they are saying. You will be constantly distracted by your worries, but if you keep going back to the words of the prayer, you will gradually discover that your worries become less obsessive and that you really start to enjoy praying.

110

And as the prayer descends from your mind into the center of your being you will discover its healing power.   —*Here and Now*, 90–91

Nothing is wanting!

Why is the attentive repetition of a well-known prayer so helpful in setting our hearts on the kingdom? It is helpful because the words of such a prayer have the power to transform our inner anxiety into inner peace.

For a long time, I prayed the words, "The Lord is my shepherd; there is nothing I shall want. Fresh and green are the pastures where he gives me repose. Near restful waters he leads me to revive my drooping spirit." I prayed these words in the morning for half an hour sitting quietly on my chair trying only to keep my mind focused on what I was saying. I prayed them during the many moments of the day when I was going here or there, and I even prayed them during my routine activities. The words stand in stark contrast to the reality of my life. I want many things; I see mostly busy roads and ugly shopping malls; and if there are any waters to walk along they are mostly polluted. But as I keep saying: "The Lord is my

111

shepherd..." and allow God's shepherding love to enter more fully into my heart, I become more fully aware that the busy roads, the ugly malls, and the polluted waterways are not telling the true story of who I am. I do not belong to the powers and principalities that rule the world but to the Good Shepherd who knows his own and is known by his own. In the presence of my Lord and Shepherd there truly is nothing I shall want. He will, indeed, give me the rest my heart desires and pull me out of the dark pits of my depression.

It is good to know that millions of people have prayed these same words over the centuries and found comfort and consolation in them. I am not alone when I pray these words. I am surrounded by countless women and men, those who are close by and those who are far away, those who are presently living and those who have died recently or long ago, and I know that long after I have left this world these same words will continue to be prayed until the end of time.

The deeper these words enter into the center of my being, the more I become part of God's people and the better I understand what it means to be in the world without being of it. —*Here and Now*, 91–93

Listen to God's voice of love

One of the tragedies of our life is that we keep forgetting who we are and waste a lot of time and energy to prove what doesn't need to be proved. We are God's beloved daughters and sons, not because we have proven ourselves worthy of God's love, but because God freely chose us. It is very hard to stay in touch with our true identity because those who want our money, our time, and our energy profit more from our insecurity and fears than from our inner freedom.

We, therefore, need discipline to keep living truthfully and not succumb to the endless seductions of our society. Wherever we are there are voices saying: "Go here, go there, buy this, buy that, get to know him, get to know her, don't miss this, don't miss that," and so on and on. These voices keep pulling us away from that soft gentle voice that speaks in the center of our being: "You are my beloved, on you my favor rests."

Prayer is the discipline of listening to that voice of love. Jesus spent many nights in prayer listening to the voice that had spoken to him at the Jordan River. We too must pray. Without prayer, we become deaf to the voice of love and become confused by the many competing voices asking for our attention. How difficult this is! When we sit down for half an hour — without talking to someone, listening to music, watching television, or reading a book — and try to become very still, we often find ourselves so overwhelmed by our noisy inner voices that we can hardly wait to get busy and distracted again. Our inner life often looks like a banana tree full of jumping monkeys! But when we decide not to run away and stay focused, these monkeys may gradually go away because of lack of attention, and the soft gentle voice calling us the beloved may gradually make itself heard. Much of Jesus' prayer took place during the night. "Night" means more than the absence of the sun. It also means the absence of satisfying feelings or enlightening insights. That's why it is so hard to be faithful. But God is greater than our hearts and minds and keeps calling us the beloved . . . far beyond all feelings and thoughts.   —*Here and Now*, 136–37

CULTIVATE PRESENCE

By presence I mean attentiveness to the blessings that come to you day after day, year after year. The problem of modern living is that we are too busy — looking for affirmation in the wrong places? — to notice that we are being blessed.

—Life of the Beloved, 64

The mystery of the incarnation

I think that we have hardly thought through the immense implications of the mystery of the incarnation. Where is God? God is where we are weak, vulnerable, small, and dependent. God is where the poor are, the hungry, the handicapped, the mentally ill, the elderly, the powerless. How can we come to know God when our focus is elsewhere, on success, influence, and power? I increasingly believe that our faithfulness will depend on our willingness to go where there is brokenness, loneliness, and human need. If the church has a future it is a future with the poor in whatever form. Each one of us is very seriously searching to live and grow in this belief, and by friendship we can support each other. I realize that the only way for us to stay well in the midst of the many "worlds" is to stay close to the small, vulnerable child that lives in our hearts and in every other human being. Often we do not know that the Christ child is within us. When we discover him we can truly rejoice.   —*Sabbatical Journey,* 71

All we need is right here

"This evil generation...asks for a sign," Jesus says in the Gospel of Luke (11:29). But what we are looking for is right under our eyes. Somehow we don't fully trust that our God is a God of the present and speaks to us where we are. "This is the day the Lord has made." When the people of Nineveh heard Jonah speak, they turned back to God. Can we listen to the word that God speaks to us today and do the same? This is a very simple but crucial message: Don't wait for tomorrow to change your heart. This is the favorable time!

The people sitting around the little table in my living room were very excited about this idea. Just being here together in the presence of God, listening to God's Word, breaking bread together and drinking the cup—this is the moment of salvation; this is the moment of God's appearance among us. All we need is *right here.*

One person, who hadn't been to our Eucharist celebration before, was deeply moved by what the readings were telling her. She was struggling with her addiction to smoking and had been feeling miserable and depressed. She said, "I can't believe this. Everything you all are talking about speaks directly to me. This is more than a coincidence. God must have called me to this place to hear this."

—Sabbatical Journey, 117

Speaking words of blessing

Even though I have been the celebrant at many weddings, every time again I feel quite nervous and anxious. There seem to be so many details that I am seldom very peaceful inside until it is over.

The celebration took place at 2:00 p.m. It was a very beautiful and festive liturgy. The Gospel from John about the great commandment to love one another prompted my words about care: care for your own heart, care for each other, and care for others.

At communion time I asked everyone to come to the front to receive the consecrated bread or a word of blessing and encouragement. Many came for a blessing, and quite a few of those who had come to receive the host came up to me later and asked for a blessing. So I have been speaking words of blessing to many people during the afternoon. I realize how deeply people are touched by simple words of reassurance, encouragement, and empowerment spoken in the Name of God.

The wedding dinner was splendid. By midnight I was exhausted and left the — by then — dancing crowd, glad to be able to have a good long rest.

—*Sabbatical Journey,* 218

Taking time to listen

After my accident a few years ago and after my experience of peace with regard to my death, I felt very open and free to welcome and spend time with those who came to visit. One of the most startling things for me about those visits was the number of people who said to me, "Henri, you are a much better pastor when you are sick than when you are healthy! Finally you are taking time to listen. You're not so preoccupied. You're not hurrying crazily from one thing to another and you are much more lighthearted! What you say now is so helpful. We really enjoy the visits!"

At sixty-three I am very aware that for me it is just a question of years, a few years. And so I sense that my aging is a time for me to be thinking of my passage to more abundant life. I want to become grateful that my life will come to completion and to anticipate sending my spirit of love to all those I cherish. I feel the need to talk about my death not morbidly, but openly, and to invite my community, my family, and my friends to be with me on the path to the end of my earthly life. I want to befriend my death.   —*Finding My Way Home,* 155–56

New life is hidden in the moment

A new beginning! We must learn to live each day, each hour, yes, each minute as a new beginning, as a unique opportunity to make everything new. Imagine that we could live each moment as a moment pregnant with new life. Imagine that we could live each day as a day full of promises. Imagine that we could walk through the new year always listening to a voice saying to us: "I have a gift for you and can't wait for you to see it!" Imagine.

Is it possible that our imagination can lead us to the truth of our lives? Yes, it can! The problem is that we allow our past, which becomes longer and longer each year, to say to us: "You know it all; you have seen it all, be realistic; the future will be just another repeat of the past. Try to survive it as best you can." There are many cunning foxes jumping on our shoulders and whispering in our ears the great lie: "There is nothing new under the sun...don't let yourself be fooled."

When we listen to these foxes, they eventually prove themselves right: our new year, our new day, our new hour become flat, boring, dull, and without anything new.

So what are we to do? First, we must send the foxes back to where they belong: in their foxholes. And then we must open our minds and our hearts to the voice that resounds through the valleys and hills of our life saying: "Let me show you where I live among my people. My name is 'God-with-you.' I will wipe away all the tears from your eyes; there will be no more death, and no more mourning or sadness. The world of the past has gone" (see Rev. 21:2–5).

We must choose to listen to that voice, and every choice will open us a little more to discover the new life hidden in the moment, waiting eagerly to be born.   —*Here and Now*, 16–17

Without "oughts" and "ifs"

It is hard to live in the present. The past and the future keep harassing us. The past with guilt, the future with worries. So many things have happened in our lives about which we feel uneasy, regretful, angry, confused, or, at least, ambivalent. And all these feelings are often colored by guilt. Guilt that says: "You ought to have done something other than what you did; you ought to have said something other than what you said." These "oughts" keep us feeling guilty about the past and prevent us from being fully present to the moment.

Worse, however, than our guilt are our worries. Our worries fill our lives with "What ifs": "What if I lose my job, what if my father dies, what if there is not enough money, what if the economy goes down, what if a war breaks out?" These many "ifs" can so fill our mind that we become blind to the flowers in the garden and the smiling children on the streets, or deaf to the grateful voice of a friend.

The real enemies of our life are the "oughts" and the "ifs." They pull us backward into the unalterable past and forward into the unpredictable future. But real life takes place in the here and the now. God is a God of the present. God is always in the moment, be that moment hard or easy, joyful or painful. When Jesus spoke about God, he always spoke about God as being where and when we are. "When you see me, you see God. When you hear me you hear God." God is not someone who was or will be, but the One who is, and who is for me in the present moment. That's why Jesus came to wipe away the burden of the past and the worries for the future. He wants us to discover God right where we are, here and now.

—*Here and Now*, 17–18

Celebrate birthdays and people

Birthdays need to be celebrated. I think it is more important to celebrate a birthday than a successful exam, a promotion, or a victory. Because to celebrate a birthday means to say to someone: "Thank you for being you." Celebrating a birthday is exalting life and being glad for it. On a birthday we do not say: "Thanks for what you did, or said, or accomplished." No, we say: "Thank you for being born and being among us."

On birthdays we celebrate the present. We do not complain about what happened or speculate about what will happen, but we lift someone up and let everyone say: "We love you."

I know a friend who, on his birthday, is picked up by his friends, carried to the bathroom, and thrown clothes and all into a tub full of water. Everyone eagerly awaits his birthday, even he himself. I have no idea where this tradition came from, but to be lifted up and "re-baptized" seems like a very good way to have your life celebrated. We are made aware that although we have to keep our feet on the ground, we are created to reach to the heavens, and that, although we easily get dirty, we can always be washed clean again and our life given a new start.

Celebrating a birthday reminds us of the goodness of life, and in this spirit we really need to celebrate people's birthdays every day, by showing gratitude, kindness, forgiveness, gentleness, and affection. These are ways of saying: "It's good that you are alive; it's good that you are walking with me on this earth. Let's be glad and rejoice. This is the day that God has made for us to be and to be together."

—*Here and Now*, 18–19

God seeks joy and laughter

Money and success do not make us joyful. In fact many wealthy and successful people are also anxious, fearful, and often quite somber. In contrast,

123

many others who are very poor laugh very easily and often show great joy.

Joy and laughter are the gifts of living in the presence of God and trusting that tomorrow is not worth worrying about. It always strikes me that rich people have much money, while poor people have much time. And when there is much time life can be celebrated. There is no reason to romanticize poverty, but when I see the fears and anxieties of many who have all the goods the world has to offer, I can understand Jesus' words: "How hard it is for the rich to enter the kingdom of God." Money and success are not the problem; the problem is the absence of free, open time when God can be encountered in the present and life can be lifted up in its simple beauty and goodness.

Little children playing together show us the joy of just being together. One day when I was very busy interviewing an artist whom I admire a lot, her five-year-old daughter said to me: "I made a birthday cake with sand. Now you have to come and pretend that you're eating it and that you like it. That will be fun!" The mother smiled and said to me: "You'd better play with her before you talk to me. Maybe she has more to teach you than I have."

The simple, direct joy of a small child reminds us that God seeks the places where there are smiles and laughter. Smiles and laughter open the doors to the kingdom. That's why Jesus calls us to be like children.

—*Here and Now,* 31–32

The blessings from the poor

Jean Vanier, the Canadian who founded a world-wide network of communities for mentally disabled people, has remarked more than once that Jesus did not say: "Blessed are those who care for the poor," but "Blessed are the poor." Simple as this remark may seem, it offers the key to the kingdom.

I want to help. I want to do something for people in need. I want to offer consolation to those who are in grief and alleviate the suffering of those who are in pain. There is obviously nothing wrong with that desire. It is a noble and grace-filled desire. But unless I realize that God's blessing is coming to me from those I want to serve, my help will be short-lived, and soon I will be "burned out."

How is it possible to keep caring for the poor when the poor only get poorer? How is it possible to keep nursing the sick when they are not getting better? How can I keep consoling the dying when their deaths only bring me more grief? The answer is that they all hold a blessing for me, a blessing that I need to receive. Ministry is, first of all, receiving God's blessing from those to whom we minister. What is this blessing? It is a glimpse of the face of God. Seeing God is what heaven is all about! We can see God in the face of Jesus, and we can see the face of Jesus in all those who need our care.

Once I asked Jean Vanier: "How do you find the strength to see so many people each day and listen to their many problems and pains?" He gently smiled and said: "They show me Jesus and give me life." Here lies the great mystery of Christian service. Those who serve Jesus in the poor will be fed by him whom they serve: "He will put on an apron, set them down at table and wait on them" (Luke 12:37).

We so much need a blessing. The poor are waiting to bless us. — *Here and Now,* 82–83

Just be there

Among the most life-giving experiences of my weeks in the hospital were the visits of my father, my sister, friends, and members of my community. They had time to spare. They had nothing more important to do. They could sit close to my bed and just be there. Especially the most handicapped were very present to me. Adam, Tracy, and Hsi-Fu came in their wheelchairs. They didn't say anything, but they were there, just reminding me that I am loved as much as they are. It seemed that they wanted to tell me that my experience in the portal of death was real and could be trusted, and by their silent presence they said to me that they might be able to keep me faithful to it. When Hsi-Fu visited me, he jumped up and down in his wheelchair, and when I hugged him, he covered my face with his kisses. He made the circle full. I wanted to come to him, but in the end it was he who came to me, as if to say, "Don't worry, I got my bath, but stay close to me so that you won't lose what you learned on your bed."

—*Beyond the Mirror*, 85–86

Become as a child

I have lost much of the peace and freedom that was given to me in the hospital. I regret it; I even grieve over it. Once again there are many people, many projects, many pulls. Never enough time and space to do it all and feel totally satisfied. I am no longer as centered and focused as I was during my illness.

I wish I were. I yearn for it. It is a yearning I share with many busy people.

Because they have nothing to prove, nothing to accomplish, Hsi-Fu and all the weak and broken people of our world are given to me to call me back, again and again, to the place of truth that I have come to know. They have no success to achieve, no career to protect, no name to uphold. They are always "in intensive care," always dependent, always in the portal of death. They can bring me in touch and hold me close to that place in me where I am like them: weak, broken, and totally dependent. It is the place of true poverty where God calls me blessed and says to me, "Don't be afraid. You are my beloved child, on whom my favor rests."

I keep being reminded of Jesus' words: "Unless you become like little children, you will never enter the kingdom of heaven" (Matt. 18:3). I realize that my accident made me, at least for a while, like a little child and gave me a short taste of the Kingdom. Now all of the temptations to leave that childhood are here again, and I am not surprised that some of my friends feel that I had more to give when I was sick than after my recuperation. However, I can no longer sit and wait for another accident to point me toward the Kingdom once again. I simply have to open my eyes to the world in which I have been placed and see there the people who can help me over and over again to become a child. I know for sure that my accident was nothing but a simple reminder of who I am and of what I am called to become.

—*Beyond the Mirror,* 86–88

Break

Our brokenness is so visible and tangible, so concrete and specific, that it is often difficult to believe that there is much to think, speak, or write about other than our brokenness. —*Life of the Beloved,* 69

As a chosen and blessed human being, Henri was also broken with psychological wounds, physical limitations, and emotional needs. His special interests in psychology and spirituality in part grew from his innate sensitivities to people and were fueled by his own emotional pain. By the time Henri reached the age of forty, he had begun sharing his anguish and joys in his writing and speaking. When he wrote The Wounded Healer, *he explicitly began to link the spiritual capacity to suffer deeply with the call to minister and care for others. Suffering and personal wounds* do not disqualify one from ministry, Henri says. The key is to make our "wounds available as a source of healing for others."

Henri later wrote from Daybreak, "After ten years of living with people with mental disabilities and their assistants, I have become deeply aware of my own sorrow-filled heart. There was a time when I said: 'Next year I finally will have it together,' or 'When I grow more mature these moments of inner darkness will go,' or 'Age will diminish my emotional needs.' But now I know that my sorrows are mine and will not leave me. In fact I know they are very old and very deep."[36]

Indeed, Henri's bouts of despair never fully dissipated. Life at Daybreak both magnified and mitigated his emotional agony. As a man who had lived alone much of his life and had become somewhat used to special treatment, he now had to show up for dinner on time and share the chores. During his first year, Henri was assigned to be Adam Arnett's assistant. Twenty-five-year-old Adam could not talk or move without assistance. Regular and severe seizures racked Adam's body, and he needed hours of daily care. Henri followed a taxing routine: wake Adam at 7:00 a.m., dress him, accompany him to the bathroom, cook for and feed him, brush his teeth, put on his coat, settle him into his wheelchair, and help ready him for a day of therapeutic and community activities. Frequently a seizure would convulse Adam's body and require that much of the routine be repeated after a mandatory nap.

Henri the celibate priest—the man who could bare his heart but by his own admission found his own bodily limitations and intimacy needs terrifying—was forced by the discipline of community life to become a loving father figure who tenderly cared for the intimate needs of one with great physical weaknesses. Henri was not unaware of this dynamic. He asked Adam's parents, "Am I romanticizing, making something beautiful out of something not beautiful at all, and projecting my hidden need to be a father on a deeply retarded person? Am I spiritualizing what is an unnatural human condition? From my intellectual and psychological formation I am able to raise these questions."[37] Adam's parents assured Henri that what he was learning from Adam, they too had experienced in their family life before Adam moved to Daybreak.

Henri began confiding in Adam, who silently listened and showed Henri what a loving heart, even one embedded in a broken body, could do.

Henri writes, "His heart, so transparent, reflected for me not only his person but also the heart of the universe and indeed the heart of God. After my many years of studying, reflecting, and teaching theology, Adam came into my life, and by his life and heart he announced to me and summarized all I had ever learned."[38]

Henri writes, "The mystery of Adam is that in his deep mental and physical brokenness he has become so empty of human pride that he has become the preferable mediator of that first love poured into his heart by God.... The peace that flows from Adam's broken heart is not of this world."[39]

At Daybreak Henri let down his guard. While he admitted his weaknesses to his large readership and following, the largess of his personality and his constant mobility and activity could often momentarily distract him from his pain. He had scores of friends, but now he saw the same ones day in and day out. Slowing down to live with the very vulnerable made him more aware of his own "less visible handicaps." Most of this was good. People who hadn't seen Henri for years recognized he was less frenetic, more at peace. But as he faced his wounds, he relied too heavily on another community member who eventually found Henri's immense emotional needs overwhelming. This temporary but devastating rejection launched Henri into an emotional breakdown. Unable to function well in the community, in 1987 he left Daybreak to live in a retreat center in Winnipeg for six months, where a daily spiritual routine and psychotherapy addressed his deep need to be physically held and emotionally affirmed. Henri returned to Daybreak, rejoined community life, and, in time, rebuilt his relationships. He resumed his writing and speaking while serving the community as pastor. Plans were begun to build Dayspring, a retreat center and chapel designed to meet the special needs of Daybreak's multifaith community and the pilgrims who traveled to Daybreak, many of whom hoped for time alone with Henri.

In 1995–96 Henri took a sabbatical after seven busy years. He learned Adam was failing, and he rushed home to be there. He couldn't stop gazing at Adam's peaceful face when Adam died. Today pictures of both Henri and Adam are displayed side by side in the Dayspring chapel, where they remain a living part of the heartbeat of Daybreak.

As you read the first group in this section, "Befriend Your Brokenness," pause if you find your heart is beating faster, tears come to your eyes, or you feel any anxiety. Most people have been taught to run from brokenness. Hide pain. Deny loneliness. Henri offers a very different invitation: embrace your weakness and let it teach you. Stop to breathe deeply and pray. You may need to stop and write or talk to a friend if something stirs your heart. That would be a good step. Henri's life was a parable of how much we really do need each other.

The second group, "Put Your Brokenness under the Blessing," is a challenge to find the peace born of a broken heart. Before you begin, hear some of Henri's words as an invocation to find a source of peace in your own broken-ness: "In Adam's name I say to you: Claim that peace that remains unknown to so many and make it your own. I say claim it because with that peace in your heart you will have new eyes to see and new ears to hear and gradually recognize that same peace in people and places where you would have least expected to find peace."[40]

—R.L.

BEFRIEND YOUR BROKENNESS

The first response...to our brokenness is to face it squarely and befriend it.   —*Life of the Beloved*, 75

Why am I so tired?

Why am I so tired? Although I have all the time I want to sleep, I wake up with an immense feeling of fatigue and get up only because I want to do some work. But I feel extremely frustrated. I want to write, read, and respond to some people's requests, but everything requires an immense effort, and after a few hours of work I collapse in utter exhaustion, often falling into a deep sleep. I expected that I would be tired after the intense and busy summer, but now, after ten quiet days, it feels that the more I rest the more tired I become. There seems no end to it.

Fatigue is a strange thing. I can push it away for a long time, I can go on automatic, especially when there are many routine things to do. But when finally the space and time are there to do something new and creative, all the repressed fatigue comes back like a flood and paralyzes me.

I am quite possessive about my time. I want to use it well and realize some of my long-cherished plans. I can't tolerate wasting time, even though I want to write about wasting time with God, with friends, or with the poor! There are so many contradictions within me.

Hans keeps laughing at me. "You are here to relax, to turn off your busyness, but you are living your vacation as a big job!" He is right, but the distance between insight and practice is huge.

The real question for me is how to live my fatigue as an experience that can deepen my soul. How can I live it patiently and fully experience its pains and aches?

But I am not the only one who is tired. When I walk in downtown Toronto, I can see fatigue on the faces of the men and women moving quickly from one place to another. They look preoccupied, thinking about family, work, and the many things they have to do before the night falls. And when I look at the faces that appear on the television newscasts from Bosnia, Rwanda, and many other war-torn places, it feels like all of humanity is tired, more than tired, exhausted.

Somewhere I have to connect my little fatigue with the great fatigue of the human race. We are a tired race, carrying a burden that weighs us down. Jesus says, "Come to me, you who are tired and feel the burden of life. Take on my burden—which is the burden of the whole world—and you will discover that it is a light burden." It moves me deeply that Jesus says not "I will take your burden away" but "Take on God's burden."

So what is God's burden? Am I tired simply because I want to do my thing and can't get it done, or am I tired because I am carrying something larger than myself, something given to me to alleviate the burdens of others? —*Sabbatical Journey,* 13–14

Feeling abandoned

The feeling of being abandoned is always around the corner. I keep being surprised at how quickly it rears its ugly head. Yesterday I experienced that nasty feeling in my innermost being. Just raw anxiety, seemingly disconnected from anything. I kept asking myself, "Why are you so restless, why are you so anxious, why are you so ill at ease, why do you feel so lonely and abandoned?"

I called and put a message on Nathan's voice mail. Soon he called back and said that he would call again in the evening so that we could have ample time to talk.

Talking lessened my anxiety and I felt peaceful again. No one can ever heal this wound, but when I can talk about it with a good friend I feel better.

What to do with this inner wound that is so easily touched and starts bleeding again? It is such a familiar wound. It has been with me for many years. I don't think this wound—this immense need for affection, and this immense fear of rejection—will ever go away. It is there to stay, but maybe for a good reason. Perhaps it is a gateway to my salvation, a door to glory, and a passage to freedom!

I am aware that this wound of mine is a gift in disguise. These many short but intense experiences of abandonment lead me to the place where I'm learning to let go of fear and surrender my spirit into the hands of the One whose acceptance has no limits. I am deeply grateful to Nathan and to my other friends who know me and are willing to bind my wounds so that, instead of bleeding to death, I can walk on to the full life.   —*Sabbatical Journey,* 24–25

I feel lonely

A difficult day again. I feel lonely, depressed, and unmotivated. Most of the day I have been fiddling around with little things. The same old pain that has been with me for many years and never seems to go completely away.

Meanwhile I have been playing with a new fax machine, which arrived yesterday. I was able to put the pieces together by following the instructions in the booklet, and to my great surprise it worked! I drove to Flanders, a little town ten miles from Peapack, to find a stationery store and buy the right kind of paper for it.

I realize that my busyness is a way to keep my depression at bay. It doesn't work. I have to pray more. I know that I need to just sit in God's presence and show God all my darkness. But everything in me rebels against that. Still, I know it is the only way out.

A few very kind letters gave me a little light.

God help me, be with me, console me, and take the cloud away from my heart. —*Sabbatical Journey,* 101

I was living in a very dark place

After twenty years in the academic world as a teacher of pastoral psychology, pastoral theology, and Christian spirituality, I began to experience a deep inner threat. As I entered into my fifties and was able to realize the unlikelihood of doubling my years, I came face to face with the simple question, "Did becoming older bring me closer to Jesus?" After twenty-five years of priesthood, I found myself praying poorly, living somewhat isolated from other people, and very much preoccupied with burning issues. Everyone was saying that I was doing really well, but something inside was telling me that my success was putting my own soul in danger. I began to ask myself whether my lack of contemplative prayer, my loneliness, and my constantly changing involvement in what seemed most urgent were signs that the Spirit was gradually being suppressed. It was very hard for me to see clearly, and though I never spoke about hell or only jokingly so, I woke up one day with the realization that I was living in a very dark place and that the term "burnout" was a convenient psychological translation for a spiritual death.

In the midst of this I kept praying, "Lord, show me where you want me to go and I will follow you, but please be clear and unambiguous about it!" Well, God was. In the person of Jean Vanier, the founder of the L'Arche communities for mentally handicapped people, God said, "Go and live among the poor in spirit, and they will heal you." The call was so clear and distinct that I had no choice but to follow. So I moved from Harvard to L'Arche, from the best and the brightest, wanting to rule the world, to men and women who had few or no words and were considered, at best, marginal to the needs of our society.

—*In the Name of Jesus*, 9–12

When your heart is pierced

It is so hard to keep looking at life from above, from God's place. Recently my dear friend Jonas called me. With a broken voice he told me that his daughter, Rebecca, had died four hours after her birth. Jonas, his wife, Margaret, and their little son, Samuel, had been so much looking forward to the new baby. She was born prematurely but still able to live. However, it soon became clear that she would not live long. Jonas baptized little Rebecca; he and Margaret held her for a while and then it was all over.

Jonas said: "As I drove away from the hospital, I kept saying to God: 'Dear God, you gave Rebecca to me; now I give her back to you.' But it is such a pain, such a cutting away of a beautiful future, such a feeling of emptiness."

"Rebecca is your daughter," I said, "and she always will remain your and Margaret's daughter. She has been given to you for only a few hours, but those few hours are not in vain. Trust that Samuel has a sister and that Margaret and you have a daughter dwelling in God's eternal embrace. You signed her with the sign of the cross of Jesus with which Samuel, Margaret, and you have been signed, and under that sign your love will grow deeper and wider even when your heart is pierced."

We spoke a long time on the phone. We so much wanted to hold each other and cry together; we so much wanted to just be together and find some consolation in each other's friendship.

Why is this happening? So that God's glory can be revealed? It is so hard to say "Yes" to that when all is dark.

I look at Mary holding the dead body of Jesus on her lap. I think of Margaret and Jonas holding little Rebecca in their arms. And I pray.

—*Here and Now,* 80–81

All I experience is fragmentation

Recently someone said to me, "When you were ill you were centered, and the many people who visited you felt a real peace coming from you; but since you are healed and have taken on your many tasks again, much of your old restlessness and anxiety has re-appeared." I have to listen very carefully to these words. Is the glimpse beyond the mirror, real and powerful as it was, not able to keep me focused on God when the demands of our hectic society make themselves felt once again? Can I hold on to the truth of my hospital experience?

At first glance, it seems impossible. How do I keep believing in the unifying, restoring power of God's love when all I experience is fragmentation and sep-aration? The world I live in today seems no longer fertile soil in which the seed of grace can grow strong

144

and bear fruit. As I look at the many bulldozers devastating the beautiful farmland around me in preparation for all the houses to be placed one beside the other like cars in a parking lot, I know that solitude, silence, and prayer have fled with the deer. Competition, ambition, rivalry, and an intense desire for power and prestige seem to fill the air. My crib in the intensive care unit and my bed on the fifth floor of York Central Hospital seemed safe and holy places compared with the chaos of urban "development."

But then there is my own community of handicapped people and their assistants. What about them? Somehow I know that they can make the impossible possible. Because in the midst of this power-hungry milieu, our community holds so much weakness and vulnerability that God continues to remind us of the love that was shown to me in the portal of death.

—*Beyond the Mirror,* 83–85

PUT YOUR BROKENNESS
UNDER THE BLESSING

The second response to our brokenness is to put it under the blessing. —*Life of the Beloved*, 78

Broken glass

I recall a scene from Leonard Bernstein's *Mass* (a musical work written in memory of John F. Kennedy) that embodied for me the thought of brokenness put under the blessing. Toward the end of this work, the priest, richly dressed in splendid liturgical vestments, is lifted up by his people. He towers high above the adoring crowd, carrying in his hands a glass chalice. Suddenly, the human pyramid collapses, and the priest comes tumbling down. His vestments are ripped off, and his glass chalice falls to the ground and is shattered. As he walks slowly through the debris of his former glory — barefoot, wearing only blue jeans and a T-shirt — children's voices are heard singing, "Laude, laude, laude" — "Praise, praise, praise." Suddenly the priest notices the broken chalice. He looks at it for a long time and then, haltingly, he says, "I never realized that broken glass could shine so brightly." Those words

I will never forget.... They capture the mystery of my life.   *—Life of the Beloved, 82–83*

God's faithful presence

During the Eucharist this morning we talked about God's covenant. God says, "I am your God and will be faithful to you even when you won't be faithful to me." Through human history, this divine faithfulness is shown to us in God's increasing desire for intimacy. At first God was the God *for* us, our protector and shield. Then, when Jesus came, God became the God *with* us, our companion and friend. Finally, when Jesus sent his Spirit, God was revealed to us as the God *within* us, our very breath and heartbeat.

Our life is full of brokenness — broken relationships, broken promises, broken expectations. How can we live that brokenness without becoming bitter and resentful except by returning again and again to God's faithful presence in our lives? Without this "place" of return, our journey easily leads us to darkness and despair. But with this safe and solid home, we can keep renewing our faith, and keep trusting that the many setbacks of life move us forward to an always greater bond with the God of the covenant.

Nathan and I did some shopping, but we spent most of the day at our desks writing. At 7:00 p.m. we went to Peggy's home, where we had a delicious dinner and a very animated — as always with Peggy — conversation. Peggy was eager to know Nathan better, and he was very happy to tell her about his life, his vocation, and his great love for L'Arche. I could see a new and beautiful friendship emerge. A joy to behold!

—*Sabbatical Journey,* 134

The peace of Jesus found in weakness

Keep your eyes on the prince of peace, the one who doesn't cling to his divine power; the one who refuses to turn stones into bread, jump from great heights, and rule with great power; the one who says, "Blessed are the poor, the gentle, those who mourn, and those who hunger and thirst for righteousness; blessed are the merciful, the pure in heart, the peacemakers and those who are persecuted in the cause of uprightness" (see Matt. 5:3–11). See the one who touches the lame, the crippled, and the blind; the one who speaks words of forgiveness and encouragement; the one who dies alone, rejected, and despised. Keep your eyes on him who becomes poor with the poor, weak with the weak, and who is re-jected with the rejected. That one, Jesus, is the source of all peace.

Where is his peace to be found? The answer is surprising but it is clear. In weakness. Few people are telling us this truth, but there is peace to be found in our own weakness, in those places of our hearts where we feel most broken, most insecure, most in agony, most afraid. Why there? Because in our weakness our familiar ways of controlling and manipulating our world are being stripped away and we are forced to let go from doing much, thinking much, and relying on our self-sufficiency. Right there where we are most vulnerable, the peace that is not of this world is mysteriously hidden.

—Finding My Way Home, 80–82

Passage to freedom

One of the most radical demands for you and me is the discovery of our lives as a series of movements or passages. When we are born, we leave our mother's womb for the larger, brighter world of the family. It changes everything, and there is no going back. When we go to school, we leave our homes and families and move to a larger community of people where our lives are forever larger and more expansive. Later when our children are grown and they leave us for more space and freedom than we can offer, our lives may seem less meaningful. It all keeps changing. When we grow older, we retire or lose our jobs, and everything shifts again. It seems as though we are always passing from one phase to the next, gaining and losing someone, some place, something.

You live all these passages in an environment where you are constantly tempted to be destroyed by resentment, by anger, and by a feeling of being put down. The losses remind you constantly that all isn't perfect and it doesn't always happen for you the way you expected; that perhaps you had hoped events would not have been so painful, but they were; or that you expected something from certain relationships that never materialized. You find yourself disillusioned with the irrevocable personal losses: your health, your lover, your job, your hope, your dream. Your whole life is filled with losses, endless losses. And every time there are losses there are choices to be made. You choose to live your losses as passages to anger, blame, hatred, depression, and resentment, or you choose to let these losses be passages to something new, something wider, and deeper. The question is not how to avoid loss and make it not happen, but how to choose it as a passage, as an exodus to greater life and freedom.

—*Finding My Way Home*, 135–37

Vulnerability and openness

We are living in a culture that measures the value of the human person by degrees of success and productivity. What is your title? How much money do you make? How many friends do you have? What are your accomplishments? How busy are you? What do your children do? But it is important for us to remember that as we grow older our ability to succeed in this way gradually diminishes. We lose our titles, our friends, our accomplishments, and our ability to do many things, because we begin to feel weaker, more vulnerable, and more dependent. If we continue to look at ourselves from the point of view of success, our condition is not a good one! Because of our strong cultural vision, it is a huge challenge to look at vulnerability not as a negative thing but as a positive thing. Do we dare to look at weakness as an opportunity to become fruitful? Fruitfulness in the spiritual life is about love, and this fruitfulness is very different from success or productivity.

151

It is interesting to remember that fruits are always the result of vulnerability. A child is conceived when two people are vulnerable to each other in their intimacy. The experience of peace and reconciliation comes when people are very honest and compassionate with one another, when they are vulnerable and open about their mistakes and weaknesses. The seed that falls into broken ground bears much fruit. So perhaps it is wise to begin to shift our thinking. We want to move away from emulating successfulness and begin to dream about a life of fruitfulness.

When he was dying on the cross, Jesus was ultimately vulnerable. He had nothing left. Everything had been taken from him, including his dignity, and in the eyes of his culture he was a failure. But in all truth the moment of his death on the cross was his life's greatest moment, because there his life became the most fruitful one in all history. Jesus saw his life and his death as fruitful. "It is good for you that I go. I will send you my Spirit."

—Finding My Way Home, 142–44

A place to rejoice

It will always remain very hard for us to embrace our suffering, trusting that it will lead to new life.

Nonetheless, there are experiences that demonstrate the truth of the way that Jesus shows. Let us look at just one.

A few years ago Bob, the husband of a friend of mine, died suddenly from a heart attack. My friend decided to keep her two young children away from the funeral. She thought: "It will be too hard for them to see their father put in the ground."

For years after Bob's death, the cemetery remained a fearful and dangerous place for them. Then, one day, my friend asked me to visit the grave with her and invited the children to come along. The elder was too afraid to go, but the younger decided to come with us. When we came to the place where Bob was buried, the three of us sat down on the grass around the stone engraved with the words: "A kind and gentle man." As we sat, we reminisced about Bob.

I said: "Maybe one day we should have a picnic here.... This is not only a place to think about death, but also a place to rejoice in our life. I think Bob will be most honored when we find new strength, here, to live." At first it seemed a strange idea: having a meal on top of a tombstone. But isn't that what Jesus told his disciples to do when he asked them to share bread and wine in his memory?

153

A few days later, my friend took her elder child to the grave. Her younger brother had convinced her that there was nothing to fear.

Now they often go to the cemetery and tell each other stories about Bob. No longer is Bob a stranger. He has become a new friend and having a picnic on his grave has become something to look forward to ... at least when nobody is watching!

The tears of grief and the tears of joy shouldn't be too far apart. As we befriend our pain — or, in the words of Jesus, "take up our cross" —we discover that the resurrection is, indeed, close at hand.

—*Here and Now,* 39–40

The gift of self-confrontation

Sometimes a life of compassion offers a gift you are not so eager to receive: the gift of self-confrontation. The poor in Peru confronted me with my impatience and my deep-seated need for efficiency and control. The handicapped in Daybreak keep confronting me with my fear of rejection, my hunger for affirmation, and my never-decreasing search for affection.

I remember quite vividly one such moment of self-confrontation. During a lecture trip to Texas, I had bought a large cowboy hat for Raymond, one of the handicapped members of the house in which I lived. I looked forward to coming home and giving him my gift.

But when Raymond, whose needs for attention and affirmation were as boundless as my own, saw my gift, he started yelling at me: "I don't need your silly gift. I have enough gifts. I have no place for them in my room. My walls are already full. You better keep your gift. I don't need it." His words opened a deep wound in me. He made me realize that I *wanted* to be his friend, but instead of spending time with him and offering him my attention, I had given him an expensive gift. Raymond's angry response to the Texan hat confronted me with my inability to enter into a personal relationship with him and develop a real friendship. The hat, instead of being seen as an expression of friendship, was seen as a substitute for it.

Obviously, all of this didn't happen consciously on my side or on Raymond's side. But when Raymond's outburst brought me to tears I realized that my tears were, most of all, tears about my own inner brokenness.

This self-confrontation too is a gift of the compassionate life. It is a gift very hard to receive, but a gift that can teach us much and help us in our own search for wholeness and holiness. —*Here and Now, 99–100*

Give

In the giving it becomes clear that we are chosen, blessed, and broken not simply for our own sakes, but so that all we live finds its final significance in its being lived for others.   —*Life of the Beloved*, 84

Henri was unfailingly generous. He donated significant sums to those who cared for the homeless and persons with AIDS. Henri's letters and financial records show he paid for an African man's university tuition for several years; he gave some of his students down payment and mortgage money; he sponsored a child in South America for many, many years, and he paid for car repairs when asked by friends in need. When asked, it was rare for Henri to refuse a plea for help. The list of people, causes, and organizations he supported financially shows that Henri's heart beat where he put his treasure. His giving matched his living. After his death, those who oversaw his estate established "Henri's Heartbeat Fund" to allow for random acts of generosity. They continue Henri's lavish ways of loving people.

He was also generous, almost over-generous with the gift of himself. Boxes and boxes of letters are in the archives of St. Michael's University in Toronto, where his manuscripts and papers are kept. He personally and astutely answered letters sent to him by readers seeking pastoral advice and spiritual direction. He often exhausted himself trying to find time for the many who came to visit him seeking meaningful conversations. He frequently flew across the continent on short notice to be with a friend in distress. He had that special ability to focus in on whomever he was with and genuinely with great interest ask, "Now, tell me how you are." No matter his pain or other concerns in the moment, he listened with full attention and shared remarkable insight. He could shine the high-beam intensity of his spiritual acumen on the one person he was with at any given time. Those who were comforted by his warmth nearly always returned wanting more.

To be offered by God in love for others was his highest passion. He sought to "live my vocation, which is to announce God's love for all people." His favorite image of the *joy of ministry was this: two people with full glasses of wine toasting each other in community so that what spilled over the top was their shared ministry*

At Daybreak he unearthed something better than giving: he found that helping others realize that they have something to give and offering that together is the best of all gifts. To live out this lesson, Henri began to travel with core members. Rather than leaving the community and speaking about the mentally handicapped in glowing and inspirational speeches alone, he took Bill Van Buren or another core member with him. Often the simplicity and stark communication of the core members usurped Henri or humanized the occasion with a bored yawn or yelled interruption in the middle of his lectures. But Henri learned to love the humor and spontaneity. He realized that long after people had forgotten what he had said, they would remember Bill's laugh or Trevor's toast. Most importantly, the core members would remember how they were asked to speak up, stand tall, and share of themselves. Allowing these friends, who had so often been ignored or overlooked, find their special ways of loving others was the best gift of all.

After Henri's death Bill Van Buren, the core member who traveled most with Henri, wrote a letter to him with the help of Sue Mosteller, one of Daybreak's community leaders. He wrote, "Before I met you no one ever asked me to go on a trip before. I was excited. You asked me to go to Washington because you wanted us to go together. You kept telling me it was important for us to go together like brothers, and talk about our life at Daybreak.... In the chapel you told me that my life was important and that many people loved me. No one ever told me that before. You said God loved me.... Thank you for taking me on trips. Thank you for the books and pictures you gave me. They are on the wall in my room. I miss you, Henri, and I still cry for you. Thank you for being my best friend. Love, Bill."[41]

When Henri died, two cathedrals on two continents were full for the services held for him. In a tribute to Henri at the Toronto service, Sue Mosteller spoke: "Now he has left us, and it is time for us to take responsibility for the spirituality he gave us. If we enter into the privileged and very sacred center of our hearts and hear God's Spirit who is living there, we will hear the message that Henri was sent to teach us: don't be afraid of your pain, choose to love when relationships are difficult, choose to believe when hope is flagging, help each other, step through wounded and bitter feelings to be in union with one another, forgive each other from your hearts because God is near calling each one of us, 'Beloved.'"

The final section of this volume is divided into three groupings. "Give in Life" asks you to give of yourself to the people you know and those you meet day by day. Do what *you can for those you know and receive the gifts that others offer to you. Before you finish this grouping, try to think of two tangible, simple ways you can give to someone in your life. You might put the book down and act upon them before continuing to read.*

"Give in Death" continues the theme "every day should be well lived" but takes us further by asking us to prepare for the end of life. Ask yourself: How can I live today so that my life will bear fruit even when I am gone? This book, published several years after Henri's death, witnesses to the way his earthly life, though finished, continues to give help and encouragement to others. Henri lived an extraordinary life, but it was ordinary personal gifts of flowers, love, attention, and words of affirmation and enduring wisdom that endeared him to many.

The final group of entries, "Have Heart," is an admonition to listen, speak, and act from the center of our lives. Henri reminds us that the word "courage" comes from the French word for heart, coeur. *So courage, beloved ones. Have heart.*

—R.L.

GIVE IN LIFE

First of all, our life itself is the greatest gift to give—
something we constantly forget.

—*Life of the Beloved*, 90

Given to Each Other

When we think about our being given to each other,
what comes immediately to mind are our unique talents: those abilities to do special things especially
well. You and I have spoken about this quite often.
"What is our unique talent?" we asked. However,
when focusing on talents, we tend to forget that our
real gift is not so much what we can do, but who
we are. The real question is not "What can we offer
each other?" but "Who can we be for each other?" No
doubt, it is wonderful when we can repair something
for a neighbor, give helpful advice to a friend, offer
wise counsel to a colleague, bring healing to a pa-
tient, or announce good news to a parishioner, but
there is a greater gift than all of this. It is the gift
of our own life that shines through all we do. As I
grow older, I discover more and more that the greatest gift I have to offer is my own joy of living, my own
inner peace, my own silence and solitude, my own

162

sense of well-being. When I ask myself, "Who helps me most?" I must answer, "The one who is willing to share his or her life with me." —*Life of the Beloved,* 90

Announce God's love

Today, in my prayer I return and give thanks for my "call" to the Daybreak community. I know that it is from there that I desire to live my vocation, which is to announce God's love for all people. I am deeply grateful as I become more and more convinced of my destination in God's eternal embrace. This clarity increasingly allows me to be with each person who is with me and to receive that person's goodness, beauty, and love. My challenge, as always, is to remain at home with this marvelous and mysterious God Who sent me into the world to speak and act in Jesus' Name. —*Sabbatical Journey,* 69

Free to live fully

Today I had a memorable lunch with Jim. Although I had come to Santa Fe to ask for Jim's help in my writing, our first conversation has focused on what to do with our lives between ages sixty and eighty.

For me this is an increasingly important question, which is not without anxiety. Over the years I have built up a certain reputation. People think of me as a Catholic priest, a spiritual writer, a member of a community with mentally handicapped people, a lover of God, and a lover of people. It is wonderful to have such a reputation. But lately I find I get caught in it and I experience it as restricting. Without wanting to, I feel a certain pressure within me to keep living up to that reputation and to do, say, and write things that fit the expectations of the Catholic Church, L'Arche, my family, my friends, my readers. I'm caught because I'm feeling that there is some kind of an agenda that I must follow in order to be faithful.

But since I am in my sixties, new thoughts, feelings, emotions, and passions have arisen within me that are not all in line with my previous thoughts, feelings, emotions, and passions. So I find myself asking, "What is my responsibility to the world around me, and what is my responsibility to myself? What does it mean to be faithful to my vocation? Does it require that I be consistent with my earlier way of living or thinking, or does it ask for the courage to move in new directions, even when doing so may be disappointing for some people?"

I am more and more aware that Jesus died when he was in his early thirties. I have already lived more than thirty years longer than Jesus. How would Jesus have lived and thought if he had lived that long? I don't know. But for me many new questions and concerns emerge at my present age that weren't there in the past. They refer to all the levels of life: community, prayer, friendship, intimacy, work, church, God, life, and death. How can I be free enough and let the questions emerge without fearing the consequences? I know I am not yet completely free because the fear is still there.

Jim is sixty-two years old. I am sixty-four. We both are asking the question about how we live between sixty and eighty. The difference is that Jim is bound neither by his reputation nor to any institution, so he is very free, and he loves his freedom. It's quite an experience for me to meet such a man.

Jim seems genuinely interested in my life and writing too, without having any other goal in mind except to help me to claim what is mine. He seems to have no agenda. He doesn't seem to want me to conform to any of his ideas. I trust that God put this man in my path for a good reason.

—*Sabbatical Journey,* 168

Follow the voice of love

Close to thirty people came to the morning Eucharist! It was clear that this Monday holiday permitted people to come with their families to participate in the morning's celebration.

The Gospel about the rich young man who loved Jesus and was loved by him but couldn't follow him because of his attachment to his many possessions was a real challenge for us. What seemed to impress people was the realization that this story does not imply a huge leap from everything to nothing but rather a long series of small steps in the direction of love. The tragedy for the rich young man was not that he was unwilling to give up his wealth — who would be? The real tragedy for him was that he missed something both he and Jesus desired, which was the opportunity to develop a deep and intimate relationship. It is not so much a question of detachment as it is a question of fully trusting and following the voice of love. Detachment is only a consequence of a greater attachment. Who would worry about his few possessions when invited to be intimate with the Lord of abundance, who offers more fish than we can catch and more bread than we can eat? What would have happened if the young man had said yes to

Jesus? Wouldn't he, just like the other disciples, have become a source of hope for countless people? Now he drops out of history and is never heard of again! What a loss! To follow the voice of love, step by step, trusting that God will give us all we need is the great challenge. —*Sabbatical Journey*, 173

What we give multiplies

During the Eucharist we had a very lively discussion about the Gospel of the multiplication of bread. What we give away multiplies, and what we hoard becomes less. One of the participants was especially intrigued with the thought that the multiplication of bread might in fact have been the result of people's willingness to share the little they had with their neighbors. The true miracle might have been not that Jesus made many loaves out of a few but that he called people to not cling to their own food but trust that there was enough for everyone. If this generosity would be practiced universally in our world, there would not be so many starving people. But this is also the eucharistic vision: Jesus shares his Body and Blood so that we all can become a living Christ in the world. Jesus himself multiplies through giving himself away. We become the body of Christ, individually as well as communally. —*Sabbatical Journey,* 210

Think, speak, and act generously

During the Eucharist we spoke about generosity. I was moved by Paul's words: "The one who sows sparingly will also reap sparingly, and the one who sows bountifully will also reap bountifully. Each of you must give as you have made up your mind, not reluctantly or under compulsion, for God loves a cheerful giver. And God is able to provide you with every blessing in abundance, so that by always having enough of everything, you may share abundantly in every good work" (2 Cor. 9:6–8).

I think that generosity has many levels. We have to think generously, speak generously, and act generously. Thinking well of others and speaking well of others is the basis for generous giving. It means that we relate to others as part of our "gen" or "kin" and treat them as family. Generosity cannot come from guilt or pity. It has to come from hearts that are fearless and free and are willing to share abundantly all that is given to us. —*Sabbatical Journey,* 212

Do well what you are called to do

The more I think about the human suffering in our world and my desire to offer a healing response, the more I realize how crucial it is not to allow myself to become paralyzed by feelings of impotence and guilt. More important than ever is to be very faithful to my vocation to do well the few things I am called to do and hold on to the joy and peace they bring me. I must resist the temptation to let the forces of darkness pull me into despair and make me one more of their many victims. I have to keep my eyes fixed on Jesus and on those who followed him and trust that I will know how to live out my mission to be a sign of hope in this world. —*Here and Now*, 46–47

We do not need to compete for love

If there is one notion that is central to all great religions it is that of "compassion." The sacred scriptures of the Hindus, Buddhists, Moslems, Jews, and Christians all speak about God as the God of compassion. In a world in which competition continues to be the dominant mode of relating among people, be it in politics, sports, or economics, all true believers proclaim compassion, not competition, as God's way.

How is it possible to make compassion the center of our lives? We are insecure, anxious, vulnerable, and mortal beings—always involved, somehow and somewhere, in the struggle for survival—and so competition seems to offer us a great deal of satisfaction. In the Olympics, as well as in the American presidential race, it is clear that winning is what is most desired and most admired.

Still, Jesus says: "Be compassionate as your heavenly Father is compassionate," and throughout the centuries all great spiritual guides echo these words. Compassion—which means, literally, "to suffer with" —is the way to the truth that we are most ourselves, not when we differ from others, but when we are the same. Indeed, the main spiritual question is not, "What difference do you make?" but "What do you have in common?" It is not "excelling" but "serving" that makes us most human. It is not proving ourselves to be better than others but confessing to be just like others that is the way to healing and reconciliation.

Compassion, to be with others when and where they suffer and to willingly enter into a fellowship of the weak, is God's way to justice and peace among people. Is this possible? Yes, it is, but only when we dare to live with the radical faith that we do not have to compete for love, but that love is freely given to us by the One who calls us to compassion.

—*Here and Now*, 98–99

GIVE IN DEATH

Second, we are called to give ourselves, not only in life, but in death as well.   —*Life of the Beloved*, 92

A graced time

Last night I called Cardinal Joseph Bernardin, the archbishop of Chicago, to ask him about his health. He said, "Henri, I'm so glad to hear from you. Yesterday I went back to work, half days. I am doing really well." His voice was strong and energetic. I said, "Ever since I visited you in July I've been thinking of you a lot and praying for you, and I'm so glad that you feel so well and are ready to go to work again." Then he said, "I can't tell you, Henri, how much it meant to me that you came to see me, prayed with me, and gave me some of your books. Thanks again. This truly is a time of special graces for me."

I vividly remember my visit to the cardinal in July. At that time I was at the National Catholic HIV/AIDS Ministries Conference in Chicago. The newspapers had widely reported that Cardinal Bernardin was suffering from pancreatic cancer and had undergone intensive surgery and follow-up radiation treatments. Soon after I arrived in Chicago my priest friend Bob called to say that the cardinal would like me to visit him.

I spent half an hour talking and praying with him. I was deeply moved by our conversation. He told me about Steven, who had falsely accused him of sexual abuse and had later withdrawn his accusation. It had been major news and had caused great suffering for the cardinal. After it was all over he decided to visit Steven in Philadelphia and offer him his forgiveness, pray with him, and celebrate the Eucharist. Steven, who lives with AIDS and had very hostile feelings toward the church, was deeply touched by this gesture of reconciliation. For Joseph Bernardin as well as for Steven this had been a most important moment of life, a moment of true healing.

"Now both Steven and I are severely ill, Steven with AIDS and I with cancer," the cardinal said. "We both have to prepare ourselves for death. Steven calls me nearly once a month to ask me how I am doing. That means a lot to me. We are now able to support each other."

As the cardinal was telling me this, I started to feel very close to him. He really is a brother to me, a fellow human being, struggling as I do. I found myself calling him Joseph and dropping the words "Cardinal" and "Your Eminence."

"This is a very graced time," Joseph said. "As I go to the hospital for treatment I do not want to go through the side door directly to the doctor's office. No, I want to visit the other patients who have cancer and are afraid to die and I want to be with them as a brother and friend who can offer some consolation and comfort. I have a whole new ministry since I became ill, and I am deeply grateful for that."

We spoke about death. My mother had died after surgery for pancreatic cancer, so I knew how dangerous Joseph's illness was. Although he was very optimistic and expected to survive and be able to return to his work, he was not afraid to talk about his death. As I sat with him I became deeply convinced that his illness and possible death might be the greatest gift he has to offer to the church today. So many people are dying of AIDS and cancer, so many people are dying through starvation, war, and violence. Could Joseph's illness and death become a true compassionate ministry to all these people? Could he live it as Jesus did, for others? I was so grateful that he didn't go through the back door to the hospital but through the front door, visiting the patients. I was so grateful that Steven, living with AIDS, is there to encourage him. I am so grateful that he is willing to drink the cup of sorrow and to trust that this is his finest hour.

Obviously I hope that Joseph will completely recover from his cancer, and I am very glad to know that he has returned to his work. In my view Cardinal Joseph Bernardin is one of the most significant leaders in the Catholic Church today, and I know how much his people in Chicago hope that he will be able to continue his leadership.

Still, Joseph will die someday. His illness has confronted him with the closeness of death. I pray that what he has lived this year with Steven and his own cancer will make the time ahead of him, whether short or long, the most compassionate time of his life, a time that can bear fruit far beyond the boundary of his death.　　　　　*—Sabbatical Journey, 8–10*

What do you want when you die?

A beautiful, sunny day. We left Utica at 9:00 a.m. and arrived at Jonas and Margaret's home at two in the afternoon. The long drive gave us the opportunity to talk about many things, including my community send-off and the visit of our guests over the weekend. We also spoke about illness and death. Nathan said, "Tell me what you want if you should get in a serious accident or become terminally ill." It was good to talk about this, since I had just made a "living will" and given Nathan the authority to act in my name. I told him about my gratitude for the life I have lived so far and my desire not to be kept alive artificially, or to have any organ transplant or extraordinary surgery. I said, "I do not feel any desire to die soon, but in case of an accident or serious illness I am ready to die, and I want you to feel empowered to discontinue life support when there is no real hope of recovery." "And when you die? What do you want to happen?" Nathan asked.

I thought a little and said, "I do not want to control my own funeral or burial. That's a worry I do not need! But if you want to hear my preference, then I can say this: Keep me away from a funeral home, make a simple wooden coffin in our woodery, let people say good-bye in the Dayspring chapel, and bury me in a plot at Elgin Mills Cemetery, where other members of Daybreak can also be buried. And...keep it very simple, very prayerful, and very joyful."

—*Sabbatical Journey,* 17

Each day should be well lived

How much longer will I live? Quite a few of my class-mates have died already. But my father is nearly ninety-three and in good spirits. I could live another thirty years! Do I want to live that long? Or do I hope to be united with Christ sooner?

Only one thing seems clear to me. Every day should be well lived. What a simple truth! Still, it is worth my attention. Did I offer peace today? Did I bring a smile to someone's face? Did I say words of heal-ing? Did I let go of my anger and resentments? Did I forgive? Did I love? These are the real questions! I must trust that the little bit of love that I sow now will bear many fruits, here in this world and in the life to come.

—*Sabbatical Journey,* 61

Say yes or no to love

Just as there is an eternal life, there is an eternal death, the second death. Hell is eternal death. Is this a possibility for me, for us? I felt a real resistance in me to saying yes to that question, but Jesus and his apostles give me no way out here. Eternal death is as possible as eternal life! God offers us a choice. To say yes or no to love. To offer me a choice is to respect me as a free human person. I am no robot or automaton who has no choice. God, who loves me in freedom, wants my love in freedom. That means that no is a possibility. Eternal life is not a predetermined fact. It is the fruit of our human response.

—*Sabbatical Journey*, 57–58

The death of Adam

This morning after the Eucharist, Kathy called from Toronto to tell me that Adam Arnett had had a severe setback—a possible heart attack combined with an epileptic seizure—and had been rushed to the hospital. Shortly afterwards I talked to Nathan, and I realized that Adam was dying. I wanted to fly home immediately, and Nathan encouraged me to do so.

Adam is one of the men who introduced me into the community of L'Arche Daybreak and led me into a whole spirituality of weakness which has transformed my life. Living together with Adam at L'Arche Daybreak has profoundly influenced my prayer, my sense of myself, my spirituality, and my ministry. Adam, the man who suffers from severe epilepsy and whose life has seemingly been limited because of his many disabilities, has touched the lives of hundreds of L'Arche assistants, visitors, and friends. As my friend and housemate he has reached into the depths of my heart and has touched my life beyond words.

Arriving in Toronto I was held up in immigration since I had been out of the country for so long. But finally I made it through all the checkpoints. Nathan was waiting for me and told me what he knew about Adam's situation. We drove directly to the hospital.

Rex and Jeanne, Adam's parents, greeted me, and we were happy to see each other. Several members of the Daybreak community were there to support Rex and Jeanne and to stay close to Adam in these last hours of his life.

When I walked into Adam's room, he was breathing rather regularly with the help of an oxygen mask. Ann, the person responsible for Adam's home, said,

"This morning, shortly after he was brought to the hospital, Adam's heart stopped, and the doctor declared that he had died. But after several minutes his heartbeat and breathing returned. It seemed he was not yet ready to die. I'm sure he was waiting for Rex, Jeanne, and you."

I was deeply moved to see my friend Adam lying there, obviously living his final hours with us. I kissed him on the forehead and stroked his hair.

After half an hour just looking at Adam and talking quietly with Rex and Jeanne, I invited all those in the waiting room to gather around Adam's bed. We held hands and prayed for Adam, for his parents and family, and for his many friends. After that we just sat with him, following his breathing.

An hour later Michael, Adam's brother, came. It was clear that Michael was suffering immensely, and when he saw his brother he began to cry. His father embraced him. A few minutes later, when he saw me, he threw his arms around me and cried. I held his shaking body for a long time and then went with him again to Adam's bed.

Michael is also a member of Daybreak and, like Adam, suffers from epilepsy. I asked Michael to hold the little container with sacred oil, and, while everyone gathered again, I anointed Adam's forehead and

179

both of his hands, praying fervently that God would give him the strength to make the passage to his final home in peace.

"My, my, my…brother…is going…to heaven," Michael said through his tears. "My heart is broken. My heart is broken, Father." I held him again, and we cried together.

Around 6:00 p.m. Nathan and I went to the Church Street House to fetch the food that the assistants had prepared for Jeanne and Rex, and then we had a quiet supper at a nearby restaurant.

When we returned to the hospital, Adam was in a different room because he no longer needed the heart monitors. Adam was now close to death, and the only thing to do was to make him as comfortable as possible. He was still wearing a face mask to help his breathing, but it seemed to make little difference. Finally Rex and Ann removed the mask so that Adam could be free from all unnecessary support systems. His breathing was slow and deep; once in a while it stopped but then started again. Now he was clearly struggling. Although it seemed that he was not having any pain, it was painful to see Adam fighting for every breath. Jeanne said, "With a weak heart like his, I can't understand how he can do it…it is such a struggle." Rex knelt beside the bed and held Adam's hand; Jeanne stood on the other side with her hands on his knees. I sat on the top of the bed caressing his head and hair, and once in a while holding his face between my hands.

The hours went by, and by midnight it seemed that Adam would make it through the night. Nathan and others from Daybreak had gone home, and I started to feel my own exhaustion. Ann said, "Go home now and get some sleep. Rex, Jeanne, and I will be here, and we will call you when Adam dies."

Just after I had fallen asleep at the Dayspring, Ann called and said, "Henri, Adam has died." Adam's life — and mission — had come to its end. I thought of Jesus' words "It is fulfilled." Fifteen minutes later I was back at the hospital. Adam lay there, completely still, at peace. Rex and Jeanne and Ann were sitting beside the bed touching Adam's body. There were tears, tears of grief but also of gratitude. We held hands, and, while touching Adam's body, we prayed in thanksgiving for the thirty-four years of his life and for all that he had brought to us in his great physical weakness and incredible spiritual strength.

I couldn't keep my eyes away from him. I thought, here is the man who more than anyone has connected me with God and the Daybreak community. Here is the man whom I cared for during my first year at Daybreak and have come to love so much. Here is the one I have written about, talked about all over Canada and the United States. Here is my counselor, teacher, and guide, who never could say a word to me but taught me more than anyone else. Here is Adam, my friend, my beloved friend, the most vulnerable of all the people I have ever known and at the same time the most powerful. He is dead now. His life is over. His face is still. I felt immense sadness and immense gratitude. I have lost a companion but gained a guardian for the rest of my life. May all the angels guide him into paradise and welcome him home to the embrace of his loving God.

As I looked at Adam, I saw how beautiful he was. Here was a young man at peace. A long, long suffering had come to an end. His beautiful spirit was no longer imprisoned in a body that could not help to express it. I asked myself about the deepest meaning of these thirty-four years of captivity. But that will only gradually be revealed. Now we simply have to trust and to rest. —*Sabbatical Journey,* 103–5

Live your losses

"Those who lose their life for my sake will find it," Jesus says. There is no day without many losses. If we are attentive to our inner life, we quickly realize how many times things are not happening in the way we hoped, people aren't saying what we expected, the day is not evolving as we wanted, et cetera, et cetera. All these little "losses" can make us bitter people who complain that life is not fair to us. But if we live these losses for the sake of Jesus — that is, in communion with his redemptive death — then our losses can gradually free us from our self-centeredness and open our hearts to the new life that comes from God. The real question is: "Do I live my losses for my sake or for Jesus' sake?" That choice is a choice for death or life. —*Sabbatical Journey*, 211

Death is a passage

What I appreciate as I read Scripture is that Jesus saw death, and his own death in particular, as *more* than a way of getting from one place to another. He saw his death as potentially fruitful in itself, and of enormous benefit to his disciples. Death was not an ending for him but a passage to something much greater.

When Jesus was anticipating his own death he kept repeating the same theme to his disciples: "My death is good for you, because my death will bear many fruits beyond my death. When I die I will not leave you alone, but I will send you my Spirit, the Paraclete, the Counselor. And my Spirit will reveal to you who I am and what I am teaching you. My Spirit will lead you into the truth and will allow you to have a relationship with me that was not possible before my death. My Spirit will help you to form community and grow in strength." Jesus sees that the real fruits of his life will mature *after* his death. That is why he adds, "It is good for you that I go."

If that is true, then the real question for me as I consider my own death is not: how much can I still accomplish before I die, or will I be a burden to others? No, the real question is: how can I live so that my death will be fruitful for others? In other words, how can my death be a gift for my loved ones so that they can reap the fruits of my life after I have died? This question can be answered only if I am first willing to admit Jesus' vision of death as a valid possibility for me. —*Finding My Way Home*, 127–28

Send your spirit of love to others

After a very short visit to earth the time comes for each of us to pass from this world to the next. We have been sent into the world as God's beloved children, and in our passages and our losses we learn to love each other as spouse, parent, brother, or sister. We support one another through the passages of life, and together we grow in love. Finally we ourselves are called to exodus, and we leave the world for full communion with God. It is possible for us, like Jesus, to send our spirit of love to our friends when we leave them. Our spirit, the love we leave behind, is deeply in God's Spirit. It is our greatest gift to those we love.

We, like Jesus, are on a journey, living to make our lives abundantly fruitful through our leaving. When we leave, we will say the words that Jesus said: "It is good for you that I leave, because unless I pass away, I cannot send you my spirit to help you and inspire you."   —*Finding My Way Home,* 138–39

Dying is our ultimate vulnerability

Our weakness and old age call people to surround us and support us. By not resisting weakness and by gratefully receiving another's care we call forth community and provide our caregivers an opportunity to give their own gifts of compassion, care, love, and service. As we are given into their hands, others are

185

blessed and enriched by caring for us. Our weakness bears fruit in their lives.

And dying is our ultimate vulnerability. Instead of looking at the weakness of old age as simply the experience of loss after loss, we can choose it as a passage to emptiness where our hearts have room to be filled with the Spirit of Love overflowing. It is ultimate weakness, but it is also potentially the greatest moment of our fruitfulness.

—Finding My Way Home, 144–46

Don't wait for eternal life

Eternal life. Where is it? When is it? For a long time I have thought about eternal life as a life after all my birthdays have run out. For most of my years I have spoken about the eternal life as the "afterlife," as "life after death." But the older I become, the less interest my "afterlife" holds for me. Worrying not only about tomorrow, next year, and the next decade, but even about the next life seems a false preoccupation. Wondering how things will be for me after I die seems, for the most part, a distraction. When my clear goal is the eternal life, that life must be reachable right now, where I am, because eternal life is life in and with God, and God is where I am here and now.

The great mystery of the spiritual life—the life in God—is that we don't have to wait for it as something that will happen later. Jesus says: "Dwell in me as I dwell in you." It is this divine indwelling that is eternal life. It is the active presence of God at the center of my living—the movement of God's Spirit within us—that gives us the eternal life.

But still, what about life after death? When we live in communion with God, when we belong to God's own household, there is no longer any "before" or "after." Death is no longer the dividing line. Death has lost its power over those who belong to God, because God is the God of the living, not of the dead. Once we have tasted the joy and peace that come from being embraced by God's love, we know that all is well and will be well. "Don't be afraid," Jesus says. "I have overcome the powers of death...come and dwell with me and know that where I am your God is."

When eternal life is our clear goal it is not a distant goal. It is a goal that can be reached in the present moment. When our heart understands this divine truth, we are living the spiritual life.

—*Here and Now*, 69–70

Live each day in full awareness

Some people say they are afraid of death. Others say they are not. But most people are quite afraid of dying. The slow deterioration of mind and body, the pains of a growing cancer, the ravaging effects of AIDS, becoming a burden for your friends, losing control of your movements, being talked about or spoken to with half-truths, forgetting recent events and the names of visitors — all of that and much more is what we really fear. It's not surprising that we sometimes say: "I hope it doesn't last long. I hope I will die through a sudden heart attack and not after a long, painful illness."

But, whatever we think or hope, the way we will die is unpredictable and our worries about it quite fruitless. Still we need to be prepared. Preparing ourselves for death is the most important task of life, at least when we believe that death is not the total dissolution of our identity but the way to its fullest revelation. Death, as Jesus speaks about it, is that moment in which total defeat and total victory are one. The cross on which Jesus died is the sign of this oneness of defeat and victory. Jesus speaks about his death as being "lifted up." Lifted up on the cross as well as lifted up in the resurrection. Jesus wants our death to be like his, a death in which the world banishes us but God welcomes us home.

How, then, do we prepare ourselves for death? By living each day in the full awareness of being children of God, whose love is stronger than death. Speculations and concerns about the final days of our life are useless, but making each day into a celebration of our belovedness as sons and daughters of God will allow us to live our final days, whether short or long, as birthing days. The pains of dying are labor pains. Through them, we leave the womb of this world and are born to the fullness of children of God.

John says it clearly: "My dear friends, you must see what great love the Father has lavished on us by letting us be called God's children — which is what we are! — we are already God's children, but what we shall be in the future has not yet been revealed. We are well aware that when he appears we shall be like him, because we shall see him as he really is" (1 John 3:1–2).   —*Here and Now*, 139–40

Going home

Our life is a short opportunity to say "yes" to God's love. Our death is a full coming home to that love. Do we desire to come home? It seems that most of our efforts are aimed at delaying this homecoming as long as possible.

Writing to the Christians at Philippi, the apostle Paul shows a radically different attitude. He says: "I want to be gone and be with Christ, and this is by far the stronger desire — and yet for your sake to stay alive in this body is a more urgent need." Paul's deepest desire is to be completely united with God through Christ and that desire makes him look at death as a "positive gain." His other desire, however, is to stay alive in the body and fulfill his mission. That will offer him an opportunity for fruitful work.

We are challenged once again to look at our lives from above. When, indeed, Jesus came to offer us full communion with God, by making us partakers of his death and resurrection, what else can we desire but to leave our mortal bodies and so reach the final goal of our existence? The only reason for staying in this valley of tears can be to continue the mission of Jesus, who has sent us into the world as his Father sent him into the world. Looking from above, life is a short, often painful mission, full of occasions to do fruitful work for God's kingdom, and death is the open door that leads into the hall of celebration where the king himself will serve us.

It all seems such an upside-down way of being! But it's the way of Jesus and the way for us to follow. There is nothing morbid about it. To the contrary, it's a joyful vision of life and death. As long as we are in the body, let us care well for our bodies so that we can bring the joy and peace of God's kingdom to those we meet on our journey. But when the time has come for our dying and death let us rejoice that we can go home and be united with the One who calls us the beloved. —*Here and Now,* 140–41

Dying is the most important act of living

Dying is the most important act of living. It involves a choice to bind others with guilt or to set them free with gratitude. This choice is a choice between a death that gives life and a death that kills. I know that many people live with the deep feeling that they have not done for those who have died what they wanted to do and have no idea how to be healed from that lingering feeling of guilt. The dying have the unique opportunity to set free those whom they leave behind.

During my "dying hours," my strongest feelings centered on my responsibility toward those who would mourn my death. Would they mourn in joy or with guilt, with gratitude or with remorse? Would they feel abandoned or set free? Some people had hurt me deeply, and some had been deeply hurt by me. My inner life had been shaped by theirs. I experienced a real temptation to hold on to them in anger or guilt. But I also knew that I could choose to let them go and surrender myself completely to the new life in Christ.

—*Beyond the Mirror,* 64–65

A long process of dying to self

My deep desire to be united with God through Jesus did not spring from disdain for human relationships but from an acute awareness of the truth that dying in Christ can be, indeed, my greatest gift to others. In this perspective, life is a long journey of preparation—of preparing oneself to truly die for others. It is a series of little deaths in which we are asked to release many forms of clinging and to move increasingly from needing others to living for them. The many passages we have to make as we grow from childhood to adolescence, from adolescence to adulthood, and from adulthood to old age offer ever-new opportunities to choose for ourselves or to choose for others. During these passages, questions such as, "Do I desire power or service?" "Do I want to be visible or remain hidden?" "Do I strive for a successful career or do I keep following my vocation?" keep coming up and confront us with hard choices. In this sense, we can speak about life as a long process of dying to self, so that we will be able to live in the joy of God and give our lives completely to others.

—*Beyond the Mirror,* 65–66

HAVE HEART

All hearts are one

The love of God, neighbor, and self is one love.... This unity can be seen in three ways. First, when we direct our whole beings toward God, we will find our neighbor and ourselves right in the heart of God. Second, when we truly love ourselves as God's beloved children, we will find ourselves in complete unity with our neighbor and with God. Third, when we truly love our neighbor as our brother and sister, we will find, right there, God and ourselves in complete unity. There really is no first, second, and third in the great commandment. All is one: the heart of God, the hearts of all people, our own hearts. All the great mystics have "seen" this and lived it.

—*Sabbatical Journey*, 179–80

Courage is to "have heart"

During the Eucharist we spoke about courage. The word "courage" comes from *coeur*, which means "heart." To have courage is to listen to our heart, to speak from our heart, and to act from our heart. Our heart, which is the center of our being, is the seat of courage.

Often we debate current issues and express our opinions about them. But courage is taking a stance, even an unpopular stance, not because we think differently from others but because from the center of our being we realize how to respond to the situation we are in. Courage does not require spectacular gestures. Courage often starts in small corners: it is courageous not to participate in gossip, not to talk behind someone's back, not to ridicule another. It is courageous to think well of other people and be grateful to them even when we live different lives than they do. It is courageous to reach out to a poor person, to spend time with a troubled child, to participate in action to prevent war and violence, abuse and manipulation.

Often we praise prophets after they are dead. Are we willing to be prophets while we are alive?

—*Sabbatical Journey*, 220–21

The center of our being

Let me say here that by "heart" I do not mean the seat of human emotions in contrast to the mind as the seat of human thought. No, by heart I mean the center of our being where God comes to dwell with us and bring us the divine gifts of trust, hope, and love. The mind tries to understand, grasp problems, discern different aspects of reality, and probe the mysteries of life. The heart allows us to enter into relationships and experience that we are sons and daughters of God and of our parents, as well as brothers and sisters of one another. Long before our minds were able to exercise their potential, our hearts were developing trusting human relationships. And in fact I am convinced that these trusting human relationships even precede the moment of our birth. —*Finding My Way Home*, 68–69

Share God's heart

What does it mean to live in the world with a truly compassionate heart, a heart that remains open to all people at all times? It is very important to realize that compassion is more than sympathy or empathy. When we are asked to listen to the pains of people and empathize with their suffering, we soon reach our emotional limits. We can listen only for a short time and only to a few people. In our society we are bombarded with so much "news" about human misery that our hearts easily get numbed simply because of overload.

But God's compassionate heart does not have limits. God's heart is greater, infinitely greater, than the human heart. It is that divine heart that God wants to give to us so that we can love all people without burning out or becoming numb.

It is for this compassionate heart that we pray when we say: "A pure heart create for me, O God, put a steadfast spirit within me. Do not cast me away from your presence, nor deprive me of your holy spirit" (Ps. 51). —*Here and Now*, 109–10

Heart to Heart

The last time both of us saw Henri was on a mid-August afternoon a month before he died. We met him at the "Red Barn" guest house near Peapack, New Jersey, where he was staying during his sabbatical. We knocked on the refurbished barn door and were received with hugs and the immediate blast of energy that often surrounded Henri. He was in the midst of preparation for morning Eucharist. A couple of dozen people from the area would soon gather in an informal spiritual community bound together by the morning's shared prayer ritual and a fascination with and love for Henri. Otherwise the group had little in common.

Henri's homily that day was on the Assumption of Mary. That much we remember. But what remains vivid is the way Henri lifted the glass chalice and bid us each to say something from our hearts — a word, a worry, a question — before we came forward to receive the bread and wine. Henri created a holy dialogue, an exchange of spiritual energy and good will, as we gathered around a simple table in a converted horse barn.

When the service was over Henri invited us to his private room. There a reprint of Van Gogh's self-portrait hung over the neatly made bed. The room was orderly and organized, containing only his essentials: phone, chairs, and writing desk. Without pausing for breath, Henri curled up like a limber child in a chintz-covered easy chair for our time together. His legs were tucked beneath him and his arms rarely stayed in his lap. The purpose of our visit was for me to interview Henri about prayer for the journal that I served as editor, so I took the chair nearest him. Michael sat in the corner chair to his right. I had worried about what question to lead with, but it turned out not to matter. I asked a question about prayer and Henri replied, "Let me say something systematic about prayer...." For the next hour or so he spoke elegantly from the heart about prayer, ministry, gratitude, and forgiveness. I remember praying that my tape recorder was running properly. I didn't want to miss anything he said. It felt like we were receiving a gift of wisdom, time, and trust, and indeed we were, for the published interview turned out to be his last.[42]

After we finished talking, Henri drove me to the train station. (Michael was taking the car to his next appointment.) In Henri's little Honda, he trained his attention more on me than on the road. He seemed truly interested in the life of a working mother with small children. I was startled again that my life merited more than just the polite nod or acknowledgment. For those few moments Henri blessed me with his interest. He was the one asking the questions as he drove a little fast down the two-laned country road.

Years have passed, but that morning with Henri turned out to be a gift that still impels us to act in a new way. At first we understood that our task was to share what we had heard. We passed on Henri's wisdom through talks, retreats, and in sharing the interview with many individuals and groups. But then we began to understand the gift was not just about sharing Henri's insights, but about living out the truth of his words. We can't just talk about living from the heart; we want to try to live by the heart, too.

THE PARABLE OF THIS BOOK

This book is itself a parable of Henri's beliefs on community. In the final interview he gave to me, he said, "The two characteristics of community are forgiveness and celebration." He said it was important to say to those we live and work with most closely, "Thanks for being you."

That insight would turn out to be true in another way when on January 24, 2002, at the request of John Jones, now executive manager, the staff of The Crossroad Publishing Company gathered in their offices on Eighth Avenue in Manhattan for a pizza party in honor of Henri's seventieth birthday. Henri had died in September of 1996 but even years later those who both published and read his books continued to learn from his life of heartfelt honesty. When alive, Henri had visited the publishing house and liked to have the whole publishing staff — everyone who had a hand in the process — around the table. Thus, when they gathered to honor Henri, who had authored several of Crossroad's bestselling books, there were many stories to tell. John Tintera, on the marketing staff at the time, said something about Henri's heart, and the idea for this book was born. Gwendolin Herder, Crossroad's publisher and CEO, had known Henri since childhood when he visited her parents' home in Germany. She said, "I'd always been touched by his eucharistic and sacramental center. It seemed right to take the eucharistic movements Henri describes often, especially in *Life of the Beloved,* as the structure for the book." Then John Eagleson, a designer and typesetter who had worked on many of Henri's books, took on the task of selecting quotes from the Crossroad titles. A proposal was sent to the Nouwen estate, and the marketing staff announced the book.

Later, when the staff, which by this time had added Roy M. Carlisle to the editorial team, sat down and looked over the collection, they felt that something was missing. Roy, who had met Henri while working at another publishing company more than a decade before, looked at the manuscript and thought of Michael and me. Roy, a visionary editor, had been my first boss in my publishing career and had recognized my ability to take a good, raw idea and see what might make it more readable and more heartfelt. We had worked on many wonderful titles together. He remembered that Michael had studied with and taught about Henri and that we'd all been friends.

So Roy called us, but it probably wasn't the easiest call to make. Roy and I had left our previous publishing house at different times with our relationship in tatters. Years had passed. We'd bumped into each other a few times and exchanged a few e-mails, but we hadn't worked together in years. Should we?

In that final interview Henri gave to me, he said the second essential aspect to community is forgiveness: *forgiving the other person for not being God.* No one can meet all of our needs or expectations. But when we stop expecting others to be God, we can celebrate the little glimmer of God found in each of us.

When we thought about Henri and the gifts he'd given us and his example of heartfelt living even in times of brokenness, Michael and I knew we had to join the team brought together by this book. We responded positively to Roy's invitation and the work began.

Even after his death, Henri's heart again allowed a whole group of people to celebrate each others' gifts, to create a book that honors Henri's life and work, but most importantly, that points us all toward God's worldwide heart of forgiving and celebratory love. The circle created by Henri's heart remains open. We trust, dear readers, that you know that's there's plenty of room for you, too.   —R.L.

Notes

1. Henri's capacity for friendship was legendary. Michael Ford, in *The Wounded Prophet,* reports that Henri counted fifteen hundred personal friends in his circle. Ford interviewed a hundred of them for his portrait. See Michael Ford, *The Wounded Prophet* (New York: Doubleday, 1997), 73.

2. For Henri's perspective on this evening, see *Sabbatical Journey: The Diary of His Final Year* (New York: Crossroad, 1998), 202.

3. "Heart" is used in three of his book titles (*The Way of the Heart, With Burning Hearts,* and *Heart Speaks to Heart),* in several articles (e.g., "The Trusting Heart and the Primacy of the Mystical Life"), and in a number of section heads in his devotional guide, *Bread for the Journey* (including "Community, a Quality of the Heart," "Healing our Hearts through Forgiveness," "Friendship in the Twilight Zones in the Heart," "The Heart of Jesus," "Unity in the Heart of God," and "Hearts as Wide as the World"). A video production, *With Burning Hearts,* was released during his lifetime.

4. Henri's major source for this and the word study that follows is Paul J. Achtemeier, ed., *Harper's Bible Dictionary* (San Francisco: Harper & Row, 1985), 377. In summary, there are at least three biblical aspects of the human heart — *emotional, intellectual,* and *volitional:*

> The heart is the *center of emotions,* feelings, moods, and passions. A swollen heart breeds arrogance (Isa. 9:9),

which is in marked contrast to the gentle and lowly heart of Jesus (Matt. 11:29). Emotionally, the heart can be happy (Prov. 15:15) or sad (Neh. 2:2), troubled (John 12:27) or at peace (Col. 3:15). It can be courageous (2 Sam. 17:10), fearful (Isa. 35:11), discouraged (Num. 32:7), envious (Prov. 23:17), generous (2 Chron. 29:31), proud (Deut. 8:14), or pure (Matt. 5:8). It can be moved by compassion (Luke 7:13) or hardened by hatred (Lev. 19:17). The heart can burn with vitality (Luke 24:32) or grow cold with indifference (Rev. 2:4,5). "The mouth speaks the things that are in the heart" (Matt. 12:34).

The heart functions as the *intellectual source of thought* and reflection. The heart understands the things of God (Deut. 8:5), provides wisdom to rule justly and wisely (1 Kings 3:12), and discerns good and evil (1 Kings 3:9). In some scriptural translations, the word for "heart" is identified with "mind" (1 Chron. 29:9), knowledge (Eccl. 8:16), and memory (Prov. 3:3). "As a person thinks in her heart, so is she" (Prov. 23:7).

The heart also represents *the idea of volition* and conscience. The request for a pure heart is the desire for a new and more perfect conscience (Ps. 51:10). Volitionally, the heart is the part of us that *chooses* what to believe and how to act in the world. A person's character is determined by the choices of the heart. The heart can be stubborn (2 Chron. 36:13) or steady (Ps. 108:1), "desperately wicked" (Jer. 17:9) or "broken and contrite (Psalm 51), depending on its fundamental attitude and response to God. The heart is the center where intentionality, obedience, and devotion are formed. Hearts that have hardened to human need and grown cold to divine love can soften, warm, change, and be renewed or replaced through the gracious gift of God (see Ezek. 36:24–28).

5. *Finding My Way Home: Pathways to Life and the Spirit* (New York: Crossroad, 2001), 68.

6. "The Biblical Concept of the Heart," Regis College lecture notes, 1994, Teaching Materials Series, Nouwen Archives, University of St. Michael's College.

7. For further elaboration, see my thematic essay "A Matter of the Heart" in *The Holy Bible: New Century Everyday Study Edition*, ed. Joel Green and Tremper Longman III (Dallas: Word Publishing, 1996), 409.

8. "Parting Words: A Conversation with Henri Nouwen," *Sacred Journey: The Journal of Fellowship in Prayer* (December 1996).

9. *Here and Now: Living in the Spirit* (New York: Crossroad, 1994), 21.

10. *The Way of the Heart* (New York: Seabury, 1981), 77.

11. *Jesus and Mary: Finding our Sacred Center* (Cincinnati: St. Anthony Messenger Press, 1993), 31.

12. *The Way of the Heart*, 59.

13. "The Trusting Heart and the Primacy of the Mystical Life," *New Oxford Review* 53, no. 8 (October 1986): 5–14. A later version was published in *The Road to Daybreak: A Spiritual Journey* (New York: Doubleday, 1988).

14. Ibid., 6.

15. Ibid.

16. Ibid.

17. *The Return of the Prodigal Son: A Meditation on Fathers, Brothers, and Sons* (New York: Doubleday, 1992), 17–18.

18. *The Road to Daybreak*, 50.

19. *Heart Speaks to Heart: Three Prayers to Jesus* (Notre Dame, Ind.: Ave Maria, 1989), 14.

20. Ibid., 22.

21. Ibid., 41.

22. Ibid., 54, 57.

23. Merton appropriated the evocative phrase from his reading of the French Catholic scholar of Islamic mysticism Louis Massignon (*Essays on the Origins of Islamic Mysticism*, 1964). It has its roots in the mystical psychology of al-Hallaj, who said that "our hearts are a virgin that God's truth alone opens." The heart, Massignon explains, can be subdivided into four successive chambers or coverings. The "virgin" point represents the primordial point of human subconsciousness: the innermost, secret heart; the last, irreducible center; the deep apophatic stillness of the mystic's deep knowledge of God." See *Merton and Sufism*, ed. Rob Baker and Gray Henry (Louisville: Fons Vitae, 1999), 65.

24. Merton, *Conjectures of a Guilty Bystander* (Garden City, N.Y.: Doubleday, 1966), 156–58.

25. Hesychasm, which means inner peace and quiet, is the contemplative practice of praying the Jesus Prayer — "Lord, have mercy" — and associating the words with one's breath and heartbeat. It was introduced by the monks of Mount Athos and found its way into the Russian Orthodox tradition of praying without ceasing.

26. Nomura Yushi, *Desert Wisdom: Sayings of the Desert Fathers* (New York: Doubleday, 1982), 90.

27. Introduction to Timothy Ware, ed., *The Art of Prayer: An Orthodox Anthology,* comp. Igumen Chariton of Valamo, trans. K. Kadloubovsky and E. M. Palmer (London: Faber and Faber, 1997), 18.

28. *The Way of the Heart,* 59.

29. Introduction to *The Art of Prayer,* 17.

30. *The Way of the Heart,* 67–68.

31. Introduction to *The Art of Prayer,* 4. In Eastern Orthodoxy, this advanced stage of spiritual development is called *theosis,* or divinization by grace.

32. See *Life of the Beloved: Spiritual Living in a Secular World* (New York: Crossroad, 1992), where Nouwen structures his

reflections on "belovedness" around the four actions of the Eucharist: take, bless, break, give.

33. *Thomas Merton, Contemplative Critic* (San Francisco: Harper & Row, 1981), 37.

34. Robert A. Jonas, ed., *Henri Nouwen* (Maryknoll, N.Y.: Orbis Books, 1998), xv.

35. Laurent Nouwen, *Henri's Vader Vertelt,* distributed by Lannoo (Tielt), Belgium, 1996, 26.

36. *Can You Drink the Cup? The Challenge of the Spiritual Life* (Notre Dame, Ind.: Ave Maria, 1996). 33.

37. *Finding My Way Home,* 62.

38. *Adam: God's Beloved* (Maryknoll, N.Y.: Orbis Books, 1997), 38.

39. *Finding My Way Home,* 69–70.

40. Ibid., 82.

41. *Befriending Life: Encounters with Henri Nouwen,* ed. Beth Porter with Susan M. S. Brown and Philip Coulter (New York: Doubleday, 2001), 271–72.

42. "Parting Words: A Conversation with Henri Nouwen."

Henri Nouwen Literary Centre
11339 Yonge Street
Richmond Hill, Ontario L4S 1L1
nouwencentre@nouwen.net
www.nouwen.net